3 1994 01394 1296

D0742258

From A
to Zine

Building a Winning Zine
Collection in
Your Library

YA 025.289 BAR
Bartel, Julie
From A to zine

JULIE BARTEL

$38.00
CENTRAL   31994013941296

American Library Association
Chicago   2004

While extensive effort has gone into ensuring the reliability of information appearing in this book, the publisher makes no warranty, express or implied, on the accuracy or reliability of the information, and does not assume and hereby disclaims any liability to any person for any loss or damage caused by errors or omissions in this publication.

Composition and design by ALA Editions in Minion and Franklin Gothic, using QuarkXPress 5.0 on a PC platform

Printed on 50-pound white offset, a pH-neutral stock, and bound in 10-point coated cover stock by Data Reproductions

The paper used in this publication meets the minimum requirements of American National Standard for Information Sciences—Permanence of Paper for Printed Library Materials, ANSI Z39.48-1992. ∞

Library of Congress Cataloging-in-Publication Data

Bartel, Julie.
    From A to zine : building a winning zine collection in your library / Julie Bartel.
    p. cm.
    Includes bibliographical references and index.
    ISBN 0-8389-0886-1 (alk. paper)
    1. Libraries—Special collections—Fanzines. 2. Libraries—Special collections—
Underground periodicals. 3. Fanzines—United States. 4. Underground periodicals—
United States. I. Title.
    Z692.S5B367 2004
    025.2'89—dc22   2004009501

Copyright © 2004 by the American Library Association. All rights reserved except those which may be granted by Sections 107 and 108 of the Copyright Revision Act of 1976.

Printed in the United States of America

08 07 06 05 04   5 4 3 2 1

To my best friend Brooke,
without whom there
would be no City Library
zine collection

To library director extraordinaire Nancy Tessman,
with gratitude for
her vision, support, and guidance

And especially to my husband Kenny,
who makes everything possible

Thank you

CONTENTS

FIGURES

PREFACE

I've been involved with the alternative press for more than fifteen years now, first as a small-press literary publisher and then as a zinester. I started a literary magazine (called *Magic Realism*) with a friend in my senior year of high school that lasted for quite a few years, I'm proud to say, and actually grew beyond our ability to care for it. (We even made the cover of *Writer's Digest* once!) Sadly, it eventually became too much for us and we ended it, a decision I still support, but which I regret nonetheless. To fill the void, I turned my attention to the intersection of the alternative press and libraries. Thus was born (with a few twists and turns in between) the Salt Lake City Public Library Zine Collection, which is both the subject of and the inspiration for this book.

I have to say a few words about the Salt Lake City Library (we just call it the City Library) here. The City Library is an amazing place, full of incredibly talented and dedicated people. I've been here for close to ten years now, and I can honestly say it's the best library I've ever worked at. And that's saying a lot, I think, since I've been working in libraries for about as long as I can remember. I don't believe there has ever been a time (at least since I could do it legally) when I wasn't working in at least one library, and there has never been a time that I didn't intend to be a librarian. Even when I wanted to be an anthropologist and live in the Shetland Islands and write books about them, I still intended to be a librarian-anthropologist. (I thought I could work at a library in the Shetlands and write my book on the side. That way I wouldn't need as much grant money.) As it turns out, being a librarian is enough, and I've been lucky to find a place in an organization that not only supports my crazy endeavors, but actually encourages them. Which brings us back to the zine collection.

While I still have a faint and secret hope that there is another collection like ours out there somewhere, I'm fairly certain at this point that there isn't. At least,

I don't believe there is another zine collection of this size, with this range, that's open to the public, especially not one in a public library. I'm positive there isn't another book like this out there. We've ached for companionship as we've built the collection over the past eight years, and I've lost track of how many times we wished there were others like us we could turn to for a different perspective or a new approach. Numerous amazing people have helped us along the way, and their insight and knowledge have been invaluable. But we're greedy—we want more of you to join us.

In this book I've tried to pique your curiosity, to inspire you to delve into the world of zines, and to provide all the information necessary to start a collection of your own. While the information in this book comes primarily from my experience at a public library, I think it's applicable to just about any library setting; having worked in all kinds of libraries, I've done my best to incorporate ideas and concerns that might arise in those environments as well. I also hope that many of you will be inspired to start zines of your own, and that you'll send them our way and include them in your own collections. (Though I only have time to work on my own zine—*Yummy Sushi Pajama's*—sporadically, it's a source of constant delight.)

The "we" I mentioned earlier deserves an explanation at this point. For the most part, when I say "we" in this book I mean (besides myself) my friend and colleague Brooke Young, who has worked on the zine collection almost from its inception. Though a number of other library staff (notably Gentry Blackburn, Moey Nelson, and Liz Jones) have contributed a great deal to the collection, Brooke especially has been integral to its growth and success. In short, there would be no collection without Brooke. She has shaped it every step of the way, filled it with amazing creations, and kept it all going while I concentrated on this book, among other things. (In addition, she read this manuscript and offered invaluable suggestions and gentle correction. Of course, she also made fun of me when I got something wrong or said something really stupid, but I'm thankful for that as well.)

I need to thank all the zinesters who have supported the collection and whose projects continue to inspire us. Thanks also to all the people on the zinegeeks, zinelibrarians, and zinesters chat lists who answered my questionnaire, my follow-up questions, and my pleas for help. Thanks to Chris Dodge (for inspiration), Jenna Freedman (for organization), Greig Means (for just being so damn cool), and all the other zine librarians. Thanks to Jerianne and Davida, whose review zines are invaluable to us, and fun to read. Thanks to Joe Biel and Alex Wrekk at Microcosm for support and for help compiling lists of review zines, distros, and stores, and for listing us in the new edition of *Stolen Sharpie Revolution* (even though I couldn't find it).

Thanks to Frances, the best manager anyone could wish for, mostly for putting up with me, but also for all the support and encouragement (and for marshmallow fights and sno-cones, as well). And to Nancy Tessman and the rest of the City Library staff (especially my cohorts on Level 2) for continual support and good wishes. Thanks to Barbara Kwasnick, who first had the idea of a book. Thanks to Charles, my brother and sisters, and a whole bunch of other people who inspire me every day in various ways, even if they don't know it. And especially, thanks to my husband, both for expecting the impossible, and for making sure I'm able to make it happen.

Welcome to the World of Zines

But what are they? *That's the first question I'm usually asked when I start to talk about zines. My initial—and probably correct—impulse is to hand over a stack of zines and let the person asking the question decide.*

—Stephen Duncombe, *Notes from Underground*, 1997

But What Are They?

Zines (pronounced "zeen," like "bean," rather than "line") are basically small, self-published magazines that are usually (though not always) written by one person and distributed through an intricate network of individuals and collectives. The only thing that all zines have in common is that their existence is the result of passion rather than a desire for profit. Though accurate, this definition rarely satisfies the zine novice, since it fails to convey a clear understanding of the scope, breadth, and material reality of zines and zine culture. Perhaps because we've all grown up with guidelines and definitions and regulations for what is appropriate in various media, it's a struggle to accept that there are very few rules in the world of zines. We want a Definition, a definitive description, and restrictions which help us to define the boundaries. An exact, illuminating definition of "zines" is hard—if not impossible—to pin down, though; as Stephen Duncombe, author of perhaps the only scholarly work on zine culture, points out in the epigraph, it's difficult to convey their true essence without a show-and-tell session. So rather than attempting to formulate an authoritative definition, it's probably more helpful—and more accurate—to simply list some of the characteristics of zines and hope that we can come to a better understanding of what they are.

Each time I introduce the concept of zines to a group or classroom I end up answering the same questions, trying to help them understand zines by verifying what they are and can be. Even though (or perhaps because) I used the broadest terms possible to describe zines, listeners invariably seek assurance that they've understood the "correct" definition. "Can I do a zine about animals?" Yes. "What if I just took things from my journal and made them into something else. Is that a zine?" Yes. "Is it all right if I just draw pictures or cut things out of magazines?" Yes. "Do there have to be words?" No. "Can it be any shape that I want?" Yes. (After a flurry of similar questions, I usually just hand over a pile of zines and let them create their own personal definitions, but of course that doesn't work in print.)

Zines are about diversity, creativity, innovation, and expression. As a group, zines deliberately lack cohesion of form or function, representing as they do individual visions and ideals rather than professional or corporate objectives. With zines, anything goes. Anything. They can be about toasters, food, a favorite television show, thrift stores, anarchism, candy, bunnies, sexual abuse, architecture, war, gingerbread men, activism, retirement homes, comics, eating disorders, Barbie dolls—you name it. There are personal zines, music zines, and sports zines, zines about politics and zines about pop culture. There are zines about libraries (*Browsing Room, Nancy's Magazine, Library Bonnet*) and even more zines created by people that work in them (*Thoughtworm, Dwan, Transom*). (See figure 1.1.) There's even a zine just for zine librarians called, appropriately, *Zine Librarian Zine*. (See figure 1.2.)

I should make it clear right up front (in fact I should have done so sooner) that zines are *not* e-zines—that is, electronic magazines accessed through the Internet (which are briefly discussed in part 3 of this book). E-zines and zines—the terms are often used interchangeably, and incorrectly—are not the same thing, though their content is often similar. While often designated (and dismissed) as ephemera, zines spring from the desire to create a tangible material object, and the physicality of zines is what differentiates them in essential ways from their electronic counterparts. Zines are about paper and glue, staples, thread, and ink, not about HTML tags, links, and pop-ups. Creating an artifact which can be passed from one person to the next, which can be sent through the mail (the regular mail), is part of the appeal. As Duncombe so eloquently puts it, "There is something about the materiality of a zine—you can feel it, stick it in your pocket, read it in the park, give it away at a show"—that is integral to zine culture.[1]

Figure 1.1 Library-Related Zines

Zines come in all sizes and shapes, and while many are cut-and-paste, as seems to be the stereotype, others are hand-lettered (*A Renegade's Handbook to Love and Sabotage*), produced on a computer (*Low Hug*), printed on a letterpress (*Ker-Bloom*), or typed out on a manual typewriter (*Kitsch//artificial respiration*). Zinesters use handmade paper (*Brainscan*), linoleum-block prints (*All This Is Mine*), photographs (*Say Cheese*), and color collage (*Xenogenesis*) to enhance their work, and while many zines are simply folded in half and stapled in the middle, some are bound with twine (*Twenty-eight Pages Lovingly Bound with Twine*), some are held together with intricate metal wiring (*Fragile*), and some

Figure 1.2 *Zine Librarian Zine*

Figure 1.3 The Variety of Zines

employ the time-tested rubber band (*Night Ride Rambling*). (See figure 1.3.) There is infinite variety to be found in the content, format, and construction of zines, and there are no rules or restrictions to speak of. If you can imagine it and create it, you can make it into a zine.

You may be asking yourself: "Why would anyone do this? Creating a zine seems like a huge waste of time and money." Well, you're right. As I mentioned earlier, a desire for profit is not usually the motivating factor for creating a zine—which is good, because there is no profit to be made by making one. On the other hand, producing a zine requires time, money, and effort, all of which you must be willing to give in spades. But zines aren't about money (unless you count the money it will cost you to make one); zines are about making your voice heard and, especially, about defining and creating space within the dominant corporate media culture. "Zines, with all their limitations and contradictions, offer up something very important to the people who create and enjoy them: a place to walk to," writes Duncombe. "In the shadows of the dominant culture, zines and underground culture mark out a *free space:* a space within which to imagine and experiment with new and idealistic ways of thinking, communicating, and being."[2]

The author and librarian Chris Dodge describes zines as "case studies in 'do-it-yourself' culture, a forum for those who don't like what's on TV and can't stand what they read in the daily paper."[3] While the quality of individual zines may vary, each creation is invariably unique, a material representation of creativity and of the need to communicate. For zinesters, the satisfaction and gratification of communicating their vision is well worth the effort, whether they choose to seek a wide readership or not. As longtime zinester Chip Rowe explains, "they're Tinkertoys for malcontents," and while often considered (if they're considered at all) as part of an underground movement too radical for mainstream society, zines are a brilliant expression of the creative spirit.[4]

Where Did They Come From?

Zines—the word is taken from the term "fanzines" (which is itself a shortened version of "fan magazines")—have been around in one form or another for hundreds of years. Small chapbooks of Shakespeare's work; Thomas Paine's pamphlet, *Common Sense;* and the myriad leaflets published during the eighteenth and nineteenth centuries could all be considered precursors to the modern zine. "Self publishing ventures of independent spirit and vitality such as American broadsides from Revolutionary days, Russian Samizdat material, Dada and other avant garde art, social movements' magazines and manifestoes, and beat poetry chapbooks" all embody the same spirit and vision—if not physical form—of today's zines.[5] Their strongest historical connection, however, is with the science fiction fanzines of the 1930s, in which fans communicated with each other through elaborate letter columns.

While America certainly has no corner on the revolutionary pamphlet market (the number of treatises, leaflets, and brochures distributed during the French Revolution alone would argue otherwise), independent printing has been a hallmark of the American "independent spirit"—even before that spirit had a country of its own. Carl Berger, author of *Broadsides and Bayonets: The Propaganda War of the American Revolution*, notes that "from the beginning it was a war of words as well as gunpowder, with each major protagonist seeking to subvert and weaken the enemy camp with carefully prepared arguments" which were disseminated via broadsides.[6] Perhaps the most famous, Thomas Paine's *Common Sense*, illustrates just how powerful this type of literature can be. R. Seth Friedman, former publisher of *Factsheet Five*, has pointed out on more than one occasion that Benjamin Franklin himself was a zinester. "He published his own thoughts using his own printing presses. It wasn't the magazine business. He did it all on his own."[7]

Like their American counterparts, politically motivated dissidents of the Soviet Union self-published their work. "Samizdat," a Russian acronym for "self-publishers," was a term "coined by post-Stalin dissidents for the old Russian revolutionary practice" of "circulating uncensored material privately, usually in manuscript form—nonconformist poetry and fiction, memoirs, historical documents, protest statements, trial records, etc."[8] It is clear that political motivations, while not always central, have often determined the course of self-publishers, since the act of publishing itself might be seen at times as criminal, let alone the contents.

Though perhaps not the stuff of treason or sedition, schools of art such as the Dadaists were deliberately subversive, attempting to shock and unsettle middle-class sensibilities by publishing manifestos which demanded, among other things, "the right to piss in different colors."[9] "Like the participants in samizdat, the artistic rebels of Dada, particularly in the movement's beginnings in Zurich during World War I, had to resort to underground publishing in order to make ... bold statements," and many of the techniques they used are still practiced by zinesters today.[10] Dada magazines such as *Cabaret Voltaire, 291*, and *New York Dada* incorporated rants (a zine staple), *détournement* (taking something out of its appropriate context and giving it a context of one's own choosing, a practice zinesters have embraced), and collages, a near-necessity for beginning zinesters.

All these characteristics—political comment, literary and artistic expression, methods and means of form and distribution—found voice later in the beat poetry chapbooks and the political magazines and manifestos of America in the 1950s and 1960s. While their formats differed greatly—the beat poets often published exquisitely crafted chapbooks which were a far cry from the newsprint missives or handwritten manifestos of left-wing political groups—the attempt to communicate with others through self-publishing was the same.

Communication, perhaps the single motivating factor which most zinesters agree on, is the spark that generated the science fiction and fantasy fanzines of the 1930s and stimulated the spread and transformation of zines in the 1980s. In 1926 Hugo Gernsback started the first magazine devoted to publishing stories of science-based fiction, *Amazing Stories*. This magazine featured a letters column where fans debated story ideas, scientific concepts, and the credibility of the hypothetical science proposed by the magazine's featured authors. After a few issues, Gernsback "made a minor decision that changed the face of science fiction forever—he printed the full addresses of the letter writers so they could contact each other directly."[11]

As the letter column grew in popularity, it caught the attention (as a means of communication which they could adopt) of the various fan groups and associations which formed as a result of their initial contact through *Amazing Stories*. One of these early fan groups, the Science Correspondence Club, began publishing in 1930, and the first issue of *The Comet*, the group's amateur publication, also marked the first fanzine. "In those days, a science fiction reader who wanted to share his opinions and enthusiasm would shove a ten-sheet carbon paper sandwich into a typewriter and hack out a three or four page fanzine to send to other fans."[12] Fanzines sprouted across the country (and around the world) as devoted fans wrote in to discuss scientific concepts and developments, currents events, plots, characters, and, eventually, their own lives. Beloved serial stories were embellished and supplemented as fans wrote new, usually unauthorized, adventures to tide them over between installments, or to keep characters alive after a series ended.

"Like zines, the earliest fanzines were produced for personal and not financial reasons. They were predominately produced by aficionados of a certain subject, most frequently fantasy and science fiction literature, as documents to celebrate their devotion and interest."[13] The words "fanzine" and "fan-mag," both of which were used to denote these small, nonprofessional publications, also indicated their origins (as well as distancing them from "prozines" such as *Amazing Stories* and *Weird Tales*). While many fanzine writers were content to keep their amateur status, others aspired to write for the prozines, and many did, notably Ray Bradbury, Robert Bloch, and Robert Heinlein. This golden age of science fiction not only allowed for occasional transitions from fan to professional, but also tended to foster and legitimize the fan experience. By communicating with each other through amateur publications and building networks of like-minded people, fanzine writers were able to encourage, perpetuate, and contribute to a world which they felt passionately about. Fanzines were empowering and addictive and allowed individuals to ignore, if not destroy, the distinction between those who create and those who consume.

This unique form of self-expression had obvious appeal when the disaffected and disillusioned youth of the punk movement adopted it in the 1970s. "The late '60s saw a synergy between outspoken political commentary, literary experimentation, and heartfelt critiques of rock and roll music."[14] And then in the early 1970s something happened: "what was once the rebellious voice of a generation turned into the boring ol' establishment. The excitement of rock and roll turned into the oppressive doldrums of overblown stadium rock extravaganzas."[15] In response to this seeming betrayal of musical trust, a new kind of music evolved—punk—and with it came a new lifestyle, complete with politics, dress code, and zines. Having perhaps more in common with early avant-garde artists such as the Dadaists than with science fiction aficionados, punks had high ideals of revolution, of escaping the mundane, of life as performance. Their anti-corporate, do-it-yourself (DIY) lifestyle advocated circumventing the system and producing, distributing, and promoting on their own. As with music, and true to their DIY reputation, when the mainstream media failed to write and publish what they were looking for, punk kids did it themselves, producing zines which featured interviews, record reviews, travelogues, personal stories, and more.

By the 1980s zines had become a staple of the punk lifestyle. With the rise of cheap and accessible photocopying—and the spread of the personal computer—the "zine revolution" of the early 1980s really took off, and the medium exploded past the punk scene into an underground network of publishers, editors, writers, and artists. What really sparked the movement, however, as I mentioned above, was communication.

In 1982 science fiction fan Mike Gunderloy decided to simplify his letter writing by typing up a two-page tip sheet describing the many interesting fanzines he came across. This way he wouldn't have to duplicate his work when corresponding with friends, and he could save a little time (or so he thought).

He called his new creation *Factsheet Five,* after a short story by science fiction author John Brunner, and sent out a dozen copies. Within a couple of years *Factsheet Five,* perhaps the most influential zine of all time, grew into a full-size, internationally distributed magazine which listed thousands of zines and had thousands of readers. "By sending free copies . . . to the editors of zines reviewed in its pages," Chris Dodge explains, "Gunderloy fostered 'cross-pollination' not only among zinesters, but also among all sorts of mail artists, cartoonists, poets, and activists hungry for alternatives to mass-produced media."[16] These new connections between people "on the fringes" of society turned out to be quite powerful, and the underground publishing movement as we know it today was born.

NOTES

The epigraph for this chapter is from Stephen Duncombe, *Notes from Underground: Zines and the Politics of Alternative Culture* (London: Verso, 1997), 1.

1. Duncombe, *Notes from Underground,* 198.
2. Ibid., 195.
3. Chris Dodge, "Pushing the Boundaries: Zines and Libraries," *Wilson Library Bulletin* 69, no. 9 (May 1995): 26–30.
4. Chip Rowe, *The Book of Zines: Readings from the Fringe* (New York: Henry Holt, 1997), xii.
5. Fred Wright, "The History and Characteristics of Zines," www.zinebook.com/resource/wright1.html.
6. Carl Berger, *Broadsides and Bayonets: The Propaganda War of the American Revolution* (New York: Presidio, 1977).
7. David Gross, "Zine, but Not Heard," *Time,* 5 September 1994, 68–69.
8. George Saunders, *Samizdat: Voices of the Soviet Opposition* (Atlanta: Pathfinder, 1974).
9. Wright, "History and Characteristics of Zines."
10. Ibid.
11. R. Seth Friedman, "A Brief History of Zines," *The Factsheet Five Zine Reader* (New York: Three Rivers, 1997), 3.
12. Mark Frauenfelder, "Cheap Memes: Zines, Metazines, and the Virtual Press," www.zinebook.com/resource/memes.html.
13. Wright, "History and Characteristics of Zines."
14. Friedman, "Brief History of Zines," 5.
15. Ibid.
16. Dodge, "Pushing the Boundaries."

two

Zine Culture 101

The rejection of mainstream media and culture that is such an integral part of zines and underground culture leads naturally toward a separation between "us" and "them."

—Stephen Duncombe, *Notes from Underground,* 1997

A Few Generalizations

"I think the 'zine community' isn't really much of a community at all. We are people that share a similar interest in self-publishing, but in most other ways we are probably totally different. We just have one hobby in common (and maybe some sort of DIY ideals). The diversity of zine publishers is pretty amazing, from right-wing wackos to lefty socialists to fifteen-year-old brainy kids to stay-at-home moms; I don't see how you can see this 'community,' if you want to call it that, as anything but super-diverse and open-minded as a whole. You can't judge all zinesters by your interaction with a few of them." (*Dan Halligan is the circulation supervisor at the Foster Business Library at the University of Washington in Seattle. He also collects and restores full-sized pinball and arcade games. The alternative paper he helps run,* Tablet, *was the reader's choice award-winner for Best New Title in the 2001 Alternative Press Awards.*)

"I write a zine because I don't write a journal. It is my way of processing the world around me and engaging in dialogue through the mail. I feel at home in the zine community and find zines to be far better than the trendy 'reality television.' Zines are written by real people who are writing mostly about their real lives. I find this fascinating and integral for people like us, people living on the edges and margins of society, to document their lives, feelings, and experiences." (*Ailecia Ruscin, an American studies graduate student at the University of Kansas, has organized many activist conferences, including the Southern Girls Convention and the North American Anarchist Gathering, and is a board member for the Allied Media Project. Her first zine was written the summer after she graduated from high school; she started writing her current zine,* alabama grrrl, *in 1997.*)

"I have mixed feelings right now. It can be elitist at times, but really nice for the most part. Since it's such a big community that stretches across . . . well, the world, I guess, your feelings on it really depend on those you're around. Of course, there are some [zines] that I don't care for, but like I mentioned before, I develop mad zinester crushes. So far, my experience has been pretty good." (*The creator of the zine* All My Stars Are Gone *was sixteen years old in 2003, a "princess with self-cut hair who likes to wear two skirts at a time. I live in Portland, Oregon, with my mum and my little brother and our glorious cats.*")

"Part of the attraction of zines lies in their eccentricities and idiosyncracies; the inclusive, conspiratorial atmosphere they foster encourages a more diverse range of writing/publishing. Because it's so tight-knit and focused, the zine community is a buzz of letters, ideas, and opinions being bandied back and forth. Good zines are popularized through word-of-mouth and the occasional swap-meet. Readers write in with personal stories, articles, and criticisms, send weird presents, and often contribute to future issues. Other ziners exchange plugs, trade copies, and sometimes do joint issues. The grassroots atmosphere is very supportive and rewarding, encouraging localized activism and creativity." (From *Splinter* no. 1, available online at www.cse.unsw.edu.au/~peteg/ zine/splinter/splinter01/zines.html)

"There is a big divide in the zine community. There are people that have come to the zine scene from politicized communities like the punk rock scene or maybe they are activists, and they have come to see zines as a way to spread their opinions and focus their ideas. The other kind of people have come at it from a different perspective, where they are more artists than activists, and want their art to be known. Of course there is overlap, which I think is the best-case scenario, as I think that each needs the other in order to be relevant. In both cases, I find that there is a lot of talk about the zine 'community,' and little real expression of this talk, where we are more than a group of individuals. Zines are a very personal means of expression." (*Frandroid Atreides runs Great Worm Express Distribution out of Toronto and is working on a zine called* We're All Fuckin' Doomed.)

"It isn't a very close community as far as the traditional sense of the word. It is a much looser community. People who make zines often come and go rather quickly, and many zines, even if they are around for a while, can really only reach hundreds or maybe thousands of people, so it is many micro-communities that are not reliant upon each other for existence, because every single member has entirely unique motivations and means. There are micro-alliances, some of which have blossomed to include thousands of active members, such as some distros; there are meetings of members where travel is often included at conventions; and there is communication through e-mail, and many creators of zines are the biggest supporters of zines." (*Matt Holdaway edits the compilation zine* A Multitude of Voices.)

"I feel both a part of the zinester community and not. I suppose by making a zine one is a member of this community by default. I have friends who make zines, and I am friends with many people whose zines I read. Zines are not my whole life, but they're a part of it. Maybe not as much now as they used to be, but enough for me to feel linked to the community in general." (*Teri Vlassopoulos is the creator of the zine* Melt the Snow. *She lives in Toronto and works full time for an accounting firm. She likes making things.*)

A Few More Generalizations

The generalizations that I'm willing to commit to about zine culture are as follows. First, some people make zines and some people don't. That one is pretty obvious. Second, zines are made by people who feel passionately enough about whatever it is they are creating to actually create it. Third, the most distinguishing feature of zine culture, to me, is that it is participatory: in order to be part of the culture one must participate; passivity is neither encouraged nor looked upon kindly. Any other generalizations about zines, zinesters, or zine culture are just that, generalizations, and should be regarded with suspicion, if not outright hostility. Because if there's one thing about zine culture that I'm sure of, it's that no description of mine will ever do it justice.

That said, let me generalize for a moment. The "us" and "them" mentality in the epigraph for this chapter, while an accurate statement, seems a bit dramatic to me. While I'll admit that there is indeed a separation here, a divide between the mainstream and the zine scene (or between those who do zines and those who don't), that divide is easily crossed. Moreover, there's no antipathy here, just a sort of estrangement. Zine culture can be exclusive, or seem exclusive, but in reality it is unusually welcoming. In the world of zines there is definitely room for everyone, and to be a zinester there is just one requirement—one must produce a zine. Producing a zine requires actual work, and this initiation requirement is difficult enough to warrant immediate membership in the club. Really, that's it. Make a zine and—poof—you're a zinester. So, yes, the club is a little exclusive—it does have an entry requirement. And until you meet that requirement, there may well be a little "us" and "them" going on. I hope you'll look past those labels, though, because the only thing that really stands between you and them is a zine. You make a zine, you join the "us" team. Everything else, all the generalizations I'm about to make and the stereotypes I am about to perpetuate—none of it really matters. You make a zine, you're part of the culture, you're part of the zine scene, and you can draw your own conclusions about it.

Trying to describe zine culture is like trying to describe zines. It's difficult, if not impossible, to delineate a coherent culture, especially since most zinesters will passionately deny that such a thing exists. Zinesters are as individual as their creations and feel strongly about that individuality; like all people, they defy stereotypes, and are as diverse and unique as zines themselves. Having beaten that point into the ground, I think it appropriate here to make a few generalizations about zinesters that will hopefully give newcomers to the scene a place to start and make them feel more comfortable. It's hard to cross that invisible line and feel out a new group—I know from experience that zinesters can *seem* intimidating—and it can help to have at least a little descriptive foreknowledge. So while this entire chapter will be woefully inexact—full of lies and innuendos—I'll try and make some broad statements about zine culture that will hopefully give you an idea of what some zinesters are like and what sorts of things are important to some of them.

Appearance

Let's start with the most obvious consideration: appearance. Contrary to popular belief and depiction, zinesters are not easily spotted and have few common appearance characteristics. Yes, many of them are young and sport various tattoos and piercings, have colored hair, and wear punk rock, thrift store, or rock star clothes. However—and this is important—not all zinesters look like this. Most zinesters do not look like this. This fact is important because dealing with zinesters can be intimidating. They're cool, articulate, unique, motivated people, after all. But so are you and so are, potentially, the kids who will learn about zines from you. Don't assume that someone is into zines because they dress a certain way—they may have no idea what you're talking about—and don't assume they're not because they dress a certain way. Don't make assumptions based on age or gender or anything else either. Zinesters come in all ages and shapes and styles and colors. They're nerds and divas and crusty punks, girly girls, hippies, goths, and jocks. One size does not fit all, your mileage may vary, and differences in color are the result of natural pigments.

Zines are a way of expressing yourself, and sometimes appearance is another way—but sometimes it's not. Zinesters look completely normal, no matter what that means to you. To paraphrase Wednesday from the *Addams Family,* like serial killers, they look like everybody else. So don't judge. And while usually this would mean you shouldn't assume that just because someone has three rings in their face and three colors in their hair that they're a zinester, here it can mean the opposite. Just because they don't have those things doesn't mean they're not. I'll tell you a really embarrassing story to illustrate my point. (It's my penance to tell this story at every opportunity. I still cringe at the memory. I should have known better.)

ME AND THE CHEERLEADER: A SAD TALE OF WOEFUL MISJUDGMENT

We do a program each year at my library with a local high school called "Make a Racket" (see chapter 10). It's a sort of zine-based talent show where the class makes a zine together and then performs at the show, with the zine as the program book. Each student reads poetry or a journal entry, or dances, or performs a monologue—whatever they choose to share. The first year I wasn't sure what to expect, but there was a good turnout and the kids were buzzing. While waiting for the show to start, I noticed this stunningly beautiful blond girl sitting at the front of the auditorium with a group of friends. I noticed her because, aside from her appearance—cool trendy clothes, amazing blond cheerleader hair, and cheerleading outfit and pom-poms in a bag at her feet—she was laughing with her friends and looking around the crowd, waving and shouting to people as they took their seats.

The lights went out, one of the students welcomed the audience, and then the entire class performed a little introductory number on stage. As they took their seats again I noticed that the blond girl had grabbed her bag, whispered to her friends, and then ducked out. Ahh, I thought, she's just *too cool* to be sitting here watching (or heaven forbid, participating in) a cheesy variety show. She came because she had to, did her part—the minimum—and then got the hell out. She's *obviously* too cool and too popular and way too much the head cheerleader type to stay at the library on a Friday night with her dorky creative writing classmates. I wasn't really annoyed. It was just that I thought I knew what she was up to. I felt a glimmer of . . . recognition, I guess, remembering that "type" from my own high school days.

The students performed in turn and then, as the lights dimmed after a well-lit interpretive dance, I heard stomping boots clomping down the aisle behind me. I turned to look and there she was—the blond girl—only she'd changed out of the trendy clothes and into the cheerleading outfit, pom-poms and all. Then I put the stomping together with her movement down the aisle and I looked at her feet and saw she was wearing these big, black, loose-laced combat boots, completely at odds with the red and white outfit, the red and white pom-poms. She walked to the podium, set her pom-poms down on either side of her, and unfolded a piece of lined paper. She began to read (from her own zine!?) and it was amazing. Don't judge me because I'm blond and a cheerleader. I'm not the "blond girl." That's not *me*. I'm a person, not a label. I like *this* and *that* and I have real feelings. She swore. She ranted a little. She was *so cool.*

Wow. Did I ever misjudge her. She captivated the room and I wondered (though maybe just to make myself feel better) how many other people had jumped to, if not the same conclusion as me, at least some conclusion about her—had assumed they knew her because she was a blond cheerleader. I felt awful. I hadn't said a word about her to anyone, just thought snarky little comments to myself, but I felt awful. I should have known better. Of course I should have. I spend all day every day striving to treat each new patron with the same respect as the last. I really thought I was pretty good at being nonjudgmental. Apparently not so much.

I made sure to seek her out afterwards and tell her how brilliant her reading was. But I still feel bad. The only good thing to come out of the experience is that it showed me clearly that I still have my own biases—and just because I'm usually biased *toward* the people others are biased *against* doesn't make the bias any less hurtful or unrealistic. So the moral is—not that you need it spelled out for you, but here it is anyway—don't judge. Not all zinesters dress, act, or think alike. Don't assume anything. Let people surprise you. Because you just never know.

And Yet More Generalizations

"I am not a zinester. I make zines. More accurately, I am a small publisher. Identifying [myself] as a 'zinester' comes with an entire set of expectations, some of which I don't agree with and many that I don't want to be associated with. I don't want to self-identify myself as a 'zinester,' but I will be viewed as one because it is the outcome of my effort; it's the description of my craft. Knit/knitter, paint/painter, zine/zinester. I want to avoid falling victim to all the stereotypes that the label 'zinester' implies. I can avoid some of these stereotypes by concentrating on the act of making zines, and introducing as many people to the zine genre as possible." (*A. J. Michel publishes the zine* Low Hug. *She is currently in the process of moving to Canada.*)

"I can't really say that I have a tidy label at this point in my life. I'm thirty-one and have been a professional activist, which was somewhat separate from my zines. I have piercings and a tattoo, but if I wanted to could pass for an office worker . . . Zines are often a reflection of who you are as a person. You might see a kid with a mohawk and try and sum him up as punk, only to find out in his zine that he plays classical violin. In my experience zines often allow you to try on different labels until you figure out who you are as a person. After that the labels tend to fall by the wayside." (*Davida Gypsy Breier is the editor of* Xerography Debt *zine and author of the zine* Leeking Ink. *Her column "Bastard Spawn" on the Atomic Books website offers tips and resources for zine makers. She is also the coauthor of the book* Vegan and Vegetarian FAQ.)

"I used to characterize myself into various subcultures but I felt that it only limited my person. How about 'zinester'. . . It's a tricky thing. Some people want to put me in a box because I listen to a hip-hop record or ride my bike as transportation. It creates a certain amount of expectation. Imagine going to a zine gathering assuming everyone is going to be punks or activists. It creates a certain expectation on your part. I feel another, larger, problem is people assuming that their subculture created zines or gives them widespread credibility—as in punks, riot grrrls, or activists. Zines have been around longer than anything but the latter." (*Joe Biel runs Microcosm Publishing and is the author of the zine* The CIA Makes Science Fiction Unexciting.)

"I'm really not sure if I fit any labels right now. I suppose I do still identify with the punk rock movement, even though I rarely participate actively in it anymore. At one time, though, I was fairly active in it, at least from a musical standpoint. I think that I share many activist viewpoints, but I wouldn't call myself an activist. I believe in acting out my politics on mostly a personal level. For example, I'm vegan and right now I'm commuting to work on my bicycle. Those are two things that I feel are important, and they also make statements that people sometimes want to discuss with me." (*Sean Stewart is a public librarian in northern Texas. He likes cooking vegan food and riding his bike and has been publishing his zine* Thoughtworm *since 1996. He also writes online zine reviews for NewPages.com and cowrites zine reviews with his partner Malinda for* A Reader's Guide to the Underground Press.)

"I don't know if I'm really any one thing. I'm vegan, I'm a little nerdy, I like weird, funny stuff. I like to do stuff myself. I don't really consider myself an activist, but there are things I care about like animal rights and such . . . Zine culture is very DIY and many of the people seem very frugal, because you kind of have to be if you don't want to go completely broke. So I found we all kind of have the same mind-set—DIY people who don't like to waste, trying to get by and get our words out there." (*Stephanie Scarborough is vegan, addicted to cookbooks, and the author of* The Cheap Vegan *and* The Rabbit Fodder Addict *zines. She's also addicted to rice cakes and wishes she could play the accordion.*)

What Zinesters Have in Common

Having said that not all zinesters look alike or are alike, that they are all into different things and really have very little in common, let me tell you what they do have in common. Mind you, the following section is a complete generalization, and only applies to zinesters in a general, nonspecific way. But in the interest of introducing zine culture, there are a couple of topics, concerns, and attitudes that surface repeatedly on chat lists, or in conversation, or in the zines themselves. I've narrowed the list down to the bare basics and come up with the following things that I think many, or at least some, zinesters have an interest in: music, politics and activism, self-expression and self-therapy, and DIY.

Music

As mentioned in chapter 1, zines as we know and love them today really first blossomed during the punk heyday of the 1970s, so the current zine scene's love affair with music should come as no surprise. Music has been an intrinsic part of zine culture for a long time, whether as the inspiration and subject of the publications themselves, or simply as an integral part of the creators' lifestyle. I don't think it's overstating the fact to say that a great many zines offer some kind of commentary on music—whether through band interviews, record or concert reviews, or lists of "what I'm listening to now." Mix-tape trades are informally organized on a pretty regular basis, at least on the chat lists I frequent, and many zines include homages of some kind to the mix-tape phenomenon: "songs listened to while making this zine," lists of best songs à la Nick Hornby's *High Fidelity*, etc.

Many independent performance spaces also house info shops or small zine libraries, and conversely, many, if not most, formal zinester gatherings (like fairs and conferences) offer shows as part of the schedule. (This might be because many zinesters are in bands themselves, or have close friends who are in bands.) Similarly, many distros (see chapter 6) offer a selection of music as well; some began by carrying music and now carry zines, some carried zines and added music later on. In any case, the independent music scene boasts an amazing number of small-label recordings, and zines help promote, review, and distribute these recordings in various ingenious ways.

As might be expected, musical tastes among zinesters run the gamut from pop to classical, but they lean heavily toward hip-hop, political rap, punk, emo, and alternative. As with most mainstream culture, zinesters may express disdain—in a general way—for whatever is currently popular, though on an individual level I don't think any sort of general statement about their musical tastes would be even remotely accurate. Rather than attempting to pinpoint what kind of music they listen to, let's just say they listen to a lot of it, communicate through it, and still consider it vital to the zinester lifestyle.

Activism and Politics

"So when individuals start recognizing and seizing their place in the discussion, rather than merely consuming what's dropped on their doorstep, it's not radical, it's a restoration of the printed word as it was meant to operate. And the printed word has always been political. Doing a zine, publishing anything on an individual or collective basis, basically says, 'ya, that's fine, but here's what I think, here's what I care about.'" (Hilary Clark, "Photocopied Politics: Zines (re)Produce a New Activist Culture," *Broken Pencil* no. 6, available online at www.broken-pencil.com/features/feature.php?featureid=22)

Many zinesters get into zines in the first place because they have something to say; it almost goes without saying that they often have strong opinions about everything from politics to culture to the minutiae of daily life. If they didn't, they wouldn't have much to write about. In addition—as I mentioned at the beginning of this chapter—zine culture requires participation, which automatically weeds out those whose tendency is merely to think or talk. Which leaves us with a group of opinionated, articulate people with a propensity for *doing*. It's no surprise, then, that zinesters are a politically active bunch who voice their opinions, act on their convictions (to varying degrees), and are probably more involved—as a group—in activist activities than your average man on the street.

The idea that everyone can make a difference, that every opinion or experience counts, that individuals have power, is at the core of zine culture. The act of publishing a zine is, to some extent, a political act in and of itself, and I think many zinesters are very conscious of this fact. Of course, I'm generalizing again. Lots of zinesters make zines just because it's fun, no strings attached. Still, there's no denying that many zines are politically motivated, or include political material.

Now I don't mean "political" in the sense of American politics (though that's definitely a popular subject) but in the broader sense—as in social theories, ideologies, relationships, and viewpoints. Zines often feature pieces on feminism or racism or various other isms; on gay and lesbian issues; on animal rights (and the vegan or vegetarian lifestyle); on politics in the traditional sense, including systems of government such as anarchism and socialism; on philosophy and theology, on the environment. In conducting interviews for this book, many zinesters who were expressly averse to labeling still identified themselves as feminists, or activists, or at least as socially conscious. Many consider themselves "activists" and often work for multiple causes. So while many zines contain no overtly political content, I think zinesters themselves are often more aware of political issues, and are more willing to act on their convictions. They know what's going on, they care, and they're willing to try and do something about it.

And while I think this propensity toward activism often leads to zining, the zine scene also fosters and encourages conscious political thought, producing zinesters who are hyperaware, largely because of the company they keep. On many chat lists the discussion is highly politicized and strays regularly from the subject of zines into discussions of semantics, politics, entitlement, empowerment, and all the isms you can imagine. While opinions vary wildly, for the most part zinesters are inclusive and nonjudgmental, consciously incorporating all lifestyle choices, social classes, races, and genders. They are violently against any kinds of isms or "phobias" such as racism and homophobia—except those with more positive connotations such as feminism, of course—and they have a healthy suspicion of the government, the media, and mainstream consumer culture.

Self-Help through Self-Awareness

"First, everything that happens to a zine editor becomes fodder for their writing. Even the most mundane visit to the dentist or annoying encounter with a bureaucratic clerk is magically transmuted into heroic journeys, righteous battles, and gleeful victories, the better to entertain one's readers. Consequently, whereas others often seem to go through life as mere sleepwalkers, the personal essayist remains sharply attuned to his or her environment, ever alert to the detail of plot and character, the possibilities of imagery and metaphor, as we seek to turn our lives into life stories . . . as I write my life, a lot of things become clearer than they might otherwise have been . . . [and] knowing that whatever happens you're going to get a good story out of it often helps to place one's current difficulties into perspective." (Robert Runte, "Why Publish? A Sociological Analysis of Motivation in Youth Avocational Subcultures," *Broken Pencil* no. 12, available online at www.brokenpencil.com/features/feature.php?featureid=45)

The hyper-awareness exhibited by many zinesters doesn't begin or end with the world at large, however, but with themselves. (I'm not sure if they do zines because they are hyper-aware, or if they are hyper-aware because they do zines, but I don't suppose it really matters one way or the other.) Creating a zine can be seen as an act of hubris, based as it is—at least to some extent—on the assumption that someone else wants to read about your life. But it's also a request for companionship and recognition and understanding; it implies a longing for that "I'm not the only one" moment where people connect and realize that they share some of the same experiences and emotions. I'd go so far as to say that creating a personal zine is a way for each zinester to legitimize their reality, to examine it, to make it real and profound by putting it into print and sharing it with others. Sharing and connecting are the key elements here, along with the introspection and thoughtfulness that can be a result. Or it might be the other way around. In any case, many zinesters engage in a form of self-therapy which is the direct result of the scrutiny they place themselves under.

Writing is often considered therapeutic, and a great many zines include highly personal, heartfelt, intense depictions of the writer's life, or at the very least an entertaining, mildly insightful recounting of their day-to-day experiences. The act of writing it all down, of creating a written account for the express purpose of sharing it with others, allows (or forces) the writer to step back at least a little and examine the actions and events and thoughts they're offering up for public consumption. Offering up the events of your life, and your interpretation of them, is brave, an act of generosity. But it also allows for a level of introspection and self-awareness that has to be therapeutic, has to be beneficial to the zinester in some way. While the putting-it-down-on-paper part might be decidedly painful, pouring your heart and soul into a zine resembles nothing so much (to me anyway) as a session with a brilliant therapist.

DIY

DIY, or do-it-yourself, is an increasingly popular concept, made mainstream by glossy new magazines, cable channels, and a host of programs, classes, and publications. Integral to the zine scene, the DIY ethic is also responsible for the extra goods that often accompany zines such as buttons, stickers, and patches, which zinesters include to promote their work or the work of others. Many zinesters are firm believers in the DIY lifestyle, making—and teaching others to make—soap, lip gloss, candles, bags, food, clothing—the list goes on and on.

There are more than a few zines and distros that focus solely on promoting DIY arts and crafts, offering up survival techniques, tips, tricks, and plans in order to spread the DIY ethic to others. Publications like the excellent *Book Your Own Fuckin' Life* offer contacts and guidelines for independent touring, including how to book shows for your band, where to crash, and how to get from place to place. *Cat's Claw Herbal* gives the lowdown on traditional herbal remedies that can be whipped up at home. Zines like *Firewood, Dwelling Portably, Compost This, Arts and Crafts Revolution,* and *A Rough Guide to Bicycle Maintenance*— which cover everything from building your own log cabin to living without a permanent residence—typify this zine subgenre. There's even a zine on DIY zines called *Stolen Sharpie Revolution,* which includes instructions for making a zine, but also for putting out your own record, bookbinding, silk screening, starting a distro, and more.

Underlying all this industry and instruction is the powerful concept at the core of zine culture: that anyone has the ability and everyone has the right to create meaningful content. With zines, the question is not just "why not do it myself?" Zines take it further by asking "why does someone else's work deserve more recognition or legitimacy than my own?" What makes one person's work more valid than another's? (Or more to the point, what makes your work more valid than my work?) Why should the power to publish be controlled by a small group of the rich and powerful when the means to get my voice heard are so easily accessed? My perspective is unique and important and I want a piece of the dialogue—I want to be involved and I want to do it myself. I don't think it's overstating the importance of this idea to say that zine culture rests squarely on the shoulders of the DIY tradition, that it takes most of its meaning and all of its power from this principle.

Obviously the do-it-yourself ethic is essential to zining. The predominant attitude these days is, why do it yourself when someone else will do it for you? Why produce content when there is so much already out there to be consumed? Zinesters, on the other hand, are more apt to wonder why someone else should do it for them when they can do it themselves just fine. Why would they choose to consume mainstream, corporate, homogenized content when they and their peers can create something better and more relevant on their own? It doesn't take long before the DIY mind-set moves from being the inspiration for zines to a way of life, and many zinesters are inherently—if not professed—DIYers. DIY is a way of prioritizing, a way of looking at the world and assuming that you can figure out how to do whatever needs to be done, and that you can do it yourself. On some level, understanding why this idea is so attractive is the key to understanding why people create zines.

So there you have it. My entirely unscientific but hopefully somewhat helpful guide to current zine culture. Of course, I could have boiled it all down to two things: first, don't judge people based on how they look. And second, all zinesters are different. But what fun would that have been?

Intellectual Freedom, the *Library Bill of Rights,* and Zines

Zines are a small, highly personalized subset of the alternative press. While many of the arguments for including alternative materials in libraries apply perfectly to zines, there are other more specific arguments for their inclusion as well. In order to describe zines' place in the grand scheme of alternative publishing, however, it is necessary to look a little more closely at the concept of the "alternative press," at its place in libraries, and at the value libraries should place on acquiring such materials.

Alternative to What?

"What is alternative literature about? What are its concerns? To answer these precisely would be to ascribe to the literature a homogeneity it simply does not possess. Just as there are a multiplicity of formats, a variety of publishers operating in a variety of ways, there are also thousands of authors and editors who have entered the world of alternative publishing to make their own voice heard." (Chris Atton, *Alternative Literature: A Practical Guide for Librarians* [Hampshire, England: Gower, 1996], 15)

The alternative press represents "a vital third sector of responsible opinion, expressing whatever ideas lie beyond the pale, whatever is not
accepted, not permitted, not available in the corporate and governmen-
tal mainstream. It comprises a civic sector of independent thought generated by individuals, local community groups, and non-governmental
organizations." (Charles Willet, "The State of Alternative Publishing in
America: Issues and Implications for Libraries," *Counterpoise* 3, no. 1
[January 1999]: 15)

In essence, the blanket term "alternative press" is used to identify small
press, independent, and underground publishers who produce books, periodicals, films, music, and zines on the fringes of the mainstream publishing industry. Alternative press publishers differ from mainstream publishers in many
ways, perhaps most notably in the subjects they cover and in their critical
appraisal of mainstream culture and the media that perpetuates it. For example,
alternative publications often focus on unpopular or unfamiliar political views;
sex, gender, and identity issues; concerns of race, class, and social institutions;
and other subjects and viewpoints which are frequently censored in the mainstream press. Beyond social commentary, however, the alternative press also represents various niche groups: fans of specific literary genres such as horror or
science fiction; afficionados of fringe music like punk, riot grrl, or thrash; and
individuals with highly personal fetishes and hobbies such as collecting toasters,
perfecting brownies, or exploring forbidden locations. By viewing and contem-
plating the dominant culture at arm's length, so to speak, they are able to offer
critiques and analysis of mainstream culture that are unavailable elsewhere, as
well as provide insights into phenomena that are out of the ordinary. Alternative
publications highlight the obscure, the unique, the specialized, and they celebrate the diversity and passion that make us interesting.

Alternative publishers are not only committed to providing a forum for
diverse views on diverse subjects, they are also committed to formulating and
publicizing alternatives. "Such calls to action," as librarian Chris Atton points
out, "are especially valuable in a culture where we are increasingly encouraged to
be passive spectators."[1] Alternative publishers, zinesters among them, have in
common the implicit invitation to readers to get involved, publish, and make
their own voices heard. This participatory inclusiveness is central to the spirit of
alternative publishing.

Another marked difference between alternative and mainstream publishers
is in devotion (or lack thereof) to profit. While publishers large and small are

obviously concerned with the bottom line, alternative publishers often publish despite it, rather than because of it. One of the "key element[s]" in alternative publishing "is a passionate commitment to truth as the writer perceives it, without regard to its marketability or orthodoxy," writes Charles Willet, former librarian and a strong proponent of the alternative press.[2] This commitment to "truth" supersedes concerns of marketability or profitability, and allows alternative publishers to simply print what they think, rather than analyzing the effect their words will have on their sales or profit margin. While not necessarily affecting the quality or importance of such products, this commitment at least ensures the publication of unfiltered, honest, and genuine works that offer a new and different perspective.

The Current State of the Publishing Industry

"Considered in their totality, zines and other alternative publications [aren't] the capricious ramblings of isolated cranks (though some certainly [are]), but the variegated voices of a subterranean world staking out its identity through the cracks of capitalism and in the shadows of the mass media." (Stephen Duncombe, *Notes from Underground: Zines and the Politics of Alternative Culture* [London: Verso, 1997], 2)

Without going into great detail (since there are whole books devoted to the subject), I'd like to comment on the current state of the publishing industry and its effect on material selection in libraries. Exact figures would be sadly out of date as soon as they were printed, but it's safe to say that the vast majority of publishing houses are owned by multinational, multimedia corporations and that there are few truly independent major publishers anymore. These media conglomerates control such a broad spectrum of news and entertainment sources that they have come to form a sort of "culture trust" which allows them to dominate both American culture and culture worldwide.[3]

Whether these media giants are either capable of or interested in using their immense power for good (meaning the inclusion and promotion of a wide spectrum of choices) rather than evil (meaning the inclusion of only those products and ideas which perpetuate the conglomerate itself) remains to be seen, but I don't think the indications are hopeful. What corporations call "synergy"—using cross-promotion between divisions and different media to increase visibility and sales—looks a lot like control, and the result is that we are left with fewer choices, less variety, and more imitation.

When so much money and power are at stake, the possibility that corporations will choose the untried, the unique, and the unfamiliar is slim at best. Why risk so much on something that's not a sure bet? A recent publishing industry conference covered by *Library Journal* noted that "there was little notion that publishing might have another mission besides growing the bottom line and that that mission might be cultural," and this should not be a surprising statement.[4] However, when devotion to profit is matched with an unparalleled ability to shape the dominant culture, it's a bit frightening to think about what we might be missing in terms of news, entertainment, and information. Mainstream media and publishing conglomerates control the market, flooding it with reviews and publicity for their products, while alternative publishers, with fewer resources and contacts, are hard-pressed to find markets for their publications. Given their dominance, the conglomerates are in a position to select the topics presented to us, dictate the amount and type of emphasis put on those topics, control how the issues involved are presented, and structure any resulting debate or discussion. As author Steven Harris explains in the alternative library journal *Counterpoise:* "It is apparent that an ever-increasing amount of the cultural output of our society is controlled by an ever smaller number of corporate entities and that our continued belief in the pluralism of our information pathways is untenable."[5] While I don't consider myself to be unduly suspicious, I find this near-total dominance just a little bit scary. Besides, I resent being restricted to a limited array of ideas and being expected to choose from what is presented rather than what I know is possible. It's like being offered only chocolate and vanilla when you know there are a hundred other flavors.

This is not to say that the products which corporations produce are without value. I *like* chocolate and vanilla. On the contrary, the culture that is perpetuated by mainstream publishers and media conglomerates is still culture and there is much to be admired, respected, and valued. A work created with the backing or support of the corporate environment can be just as brilliant, honest, and singular as the work the alternative publishing industry espouses. But if we limit ourselves, and by extension our patrons, to only the choices offered us by the mainstream, we are shortchanging both ourselves and them. Our mandate is to extract the best of what's available, not the best of what's easily available, or the best of what's currently popular, or the best of what we're offered at a good discount. As librarians we are expected and trusted to provide people with access to both mainstream and alternative materials, and that trust should not be taken lightly; it is the basis of our institution and—at the risk of being melodramatic—of our society.

The Freedom to Read

Here's the heavy philosophical part. (And if it doesn't make you swell with pride at our mission, if it doesn't make you feel powerful and necessary and inspired, then you might be in the wrong profession.) The American Library Association (ALA) has produced some very fine documents which clearly state our charge and our responsibilities as librarians. The *Library Bill of Rights* (and its accompanying interpretations) and "The Freedom to Read" statement are brilliant and idealistic declarations of what libraries stand for and what librarians believe is important.

The Library Bill of Rights

The first two policies in the *Library Bill of Rights* are highly relevant to our conversation about zines and the alternative press. The first policy states that "books and other library resources should be provided for the interest, information, and enlightenment of *all* people of the community the library serves." (The emphasis on "all" is my own; I'll come back to that in a moment.) The second policy affirms that "libraries should provide materials and information presenting *all* points of view on current and historical issues." Again, the emphasis is mine, as I want to stress the inclusive spirit at the heart of these statements. I think the relation of these statements to the inclusion of alternative materials in libraries is self-evident.

"The Freedom to Read" Statement

"The Freedom to Read" statement takes these concepts even further, expanding on them and adding depth and urgency to the ideas behind them. Rather than reprint the entire document (tempting though that is—it's really an amazing piece of writing), I'll just highlight and discuss some of the most applicable sections.

The statement begins by suggesting that "the freedom to read is essential to our democracy" and that we as librarians "trust Americans to recognize propaganda and misinformation" and believe "they still favor free enterprise in ideas and expression." The curtailment of freedom of expression and of free access to information "diminishes the toughness and resilience of our society." Furthermore, the wish to avoid controversy or to overlook differences is not a valid reason for excluding materials we find difficult, dangerous, or repugnant.

And then we get to the essence of the statement:

> The freedom to read and write is almost the only means for making generally available ideas or manners of expression that can initially command only a

small audience. The written word is the natural medium for the new idea and the untried voice from which come the original contributions to social growth. It is essential to the extended discussion that serious thought requires, and to the accumulation of knowledge and ideas . . .We believe that free communication is essential to the preservation of a free society and a creative culture. We believe that these pressures toward conformity present the danger of limiting the range and variety of inquiry and expression on which our democracy and our culture depend . . . We believe that publishers and librarians have a profound responsibility to give validity to that freedom to read by making it possible for the readers to choose freely from a variety of offerings.[6]

What does all this mean in practice? It means that librarians have a "profound responsibility" to provide the widest range of offerings possible. It means that *all* the voices that describe and examine the human condition must be represented in order to preserve our culture, our freedoms, and our ability to learn and choose intelligently. It means that when librarians place more emphasis on *where* ideas come from (established publishing houses versus the small press or the individual) and *how* they are presented (glossy magazine, professionally published book, or zine) than they do on the ideas themselves (and their merits), then people who look to the library to provide "all points of view" for the "enlightenment of all people" are being radically shortchanged.

The "New Idea and the Untried Voice"

Our system for material selection is generally based on whether we can establish the merit of a particular publication using various review and evaluation sources to give authority to our selection process. It may therefore seem unrealistic and naive to expect librarians to include materials in their selection pool that are not covered in such resources. Practically speaking, how is the same consideration to be paid to materials which have not been appraised by respected sources? While this question is certainly a valid one (and is discussed in further detail in chapters 4 and 6), I believe the more relevant and pressing question is, what will happen if we do not include the new and untried in our selection pool?

As "The Freedom to Read" statement describes, "creative thought is by definition new, and what is new is different. The bearer of every new thought is a rebel until that idea is refined and tested." As librarians, however, we should perhaps not be as concerned with perpetuating ideas that are "refined and tested" as we are with providing access to ideas that are new and different. Mainstream culture, and the publications that perpetuate it, is just that: mainstream. It is easily accessed and readily assessed. Non-mainstream culture, and the publications created by it, is by definition more difficult to access and to measure, but this in no way implies that it is less worthy of consideration.

Though professional publishing can give weight and respect to new ideas, we should not limit ourselves to including only new ideas which the mainstream media have deemed popular, acceptable, or worthy of promotion. To do so undermines the importance of the individual and of the idea, articulated by the American Library Association on the "Intellectual Freedom and Censorship Q&A" web page, that true intellectual freedom "encompasses the freedom to hold, receive and disseminate ideas" from all points of view, which illuminate a myriad of experiences, opinions, and realities.[7]

Those "rebellious" personalities who, for various reasons, share their experiences, opinions, and realities with us have a place in the library, and it is up to us to see that they are included. Some of them choose to use mainstream publication methods to share their work, while others choose alternative methods. But our concern should be the work, not the method of distribution, and the work should be evaluated for its contribution to the larger body of ideas, rather than for its refinement. Alternative publications can be disturbing and even unappealing in both presentation and content (besides being difficult to acquire), and librarians often shy away from material which may be *exceptionally* controversial, which they do not see an immediate need for, or which does not fit their perception of "refinement."

While this is understandable, it is unfortunate. Alternative publications are written by and speak to those who find nothing in the mainstream that reflects their reality. They are often explicit depictions of lifestyles which are far removed from and little considered by the mainstream, and they include shocking ideas, descriptions, language, and suggestions. "But is not much of life itself shocking?" asks "The Freedom to Read" statement. "We cut off literature at the source if we prevent writers from dealing with the stuff of life," and we do ourselves and our patrons a great disservice if we reject the contribution to our collections which alternative materials offer.

Another lengthy quote from "The Freedom to Read" statement is in order:

> Freedom is no freedom if it is accorded only to the accepted and the inoffensive. It is the responsibility of publishers and librarians to give full meaning to the freedom to read by providing books that enrich the quality and diversity of thought and expression . . . The freedom to read is of little consequence when the reader cannot obtain matter fit for that reader's purpose. What is needed is not only the absence of restraint, but the positive provision of opportunity for the people to read the best that has been thought . . . We here stake out a lofty

claim for the value of the written word. We do so because we believe that it is possessed of enormous variety and usefulness, worthy of cherishing and keeping free. We realize that the application of these propositions may mean the dissemination of ideas and manners of expression that are repugnant to many persons. We do not state these propositions in the comfortable belief that what people read is unimportant. We believe rather that what people read is deeply important; that ideas can be dangerous; but that the suppression of ideas is fatal to a democratic society. Freedom itself is a dangerous way of life, but it is ours.

Now, don't you feel proud to be a librarian?

NOTES

1. Chris Atton, *Alternative Literature: A Practical Guide for Librarians* (Hampshire, England: Gower, 1996), 16.
2. Charles Willet, "The State of Alternative Publishing in America: Issues and Implications for Libraries," *Counterpoise* 3, no. 1 (January 1999): 15.
3. Erik Barnouw, ed., *Conglomerates and the Media* (New York: New Press, 1997), 7.
4. Francine Fialkoff, "The Hollywoodization of Publishing," *Library Journal* 128, no. 11 (15 June 2003): 58.
5. Steven Harris, "Discourse and Censorship: Librarians and the Ideology of Freedom," *Counterpoise* 3, no. 3/4 (July/October 1999): 17.
6. Office for Intellectual Freedom, American Library Association, "The Freedom to Read," in *Intellectual Freedom Manual*, 6th ed. (Chicago: American Library Association, 2002), 201–5.
7. American Library Association, "Intellectual Freedom and Censorship Q&A," http://www.ala.org/Content/NavigationMenu/Our_Association/Offices/Intellectual_Freedom3/Basics/Intellectual_Freedom_and_Censorship_QandA.htm.

four

To Collect or
Not to Collect

The Whys and Wherefores

The Argument in Sound Bites

"The mainstream has the potential to self-pollinate to the point of monoculture. Maintenance of intellectual diversity is as crucial to our survival and happiness as that of genetic and ecological diversity. Librarians sit in a seat of control. We can seek out, demand, or stifle diversity just through our selection of materials. Can you imagine the discourse in society if we, librarians, fully upheld and took advantage of the Library Bill of Rights?" (Cheryl Zobel, "Zines in Public Libraries," *Counterpoise* 3, no. 2 [April 1999]: 5)

"Unless aggressively pursued, librarians would be fortunate to be aware of even 10 percent of the publishers publishing today. The other 90 percent remain obscure. Library collections represent only a fraction of the true diversity of books available. While a library cannot collect everything, most librarians are not even aware of many publications available in their effort to build a collection." (Byron Anderson, "The Other 90 Percent: What Your MLS Didn't Teach You," *Counterpoise* 3, no. 3/4 [July/October 1999]: 11)

"The overriding point to make here is that, since the material has been published, should it not therefore enjoy equal consideration with the publications of the mainstream? Many—probably the majority—of these publications are marginalized owing to their inability to compete in the marketplace with the conglomerate, international publishing houses. By choosing to ignore or by remaining ignorant of such publications we cannot but disadvantage our users. By denying them even the opportunity to become aware that such literature exists we are surely failing those who" depend upon us for information. (Chris Atton, "Beyond the Mainstream: Examining Alternative Sources for Stock Selection," *Library Review* 43, no. 4 [1994]: 59)

"There is a persistent myth that publications from small presses are the leftovers or rejects screened out by the 'rigorous' editorial standards set by editors at mainstream presses. If a manuscript can't cut it with the big houses, the authors submit to the smaller houses. With some exceptions, this is simply not true. In mainstream presses, decisions to print are market-based, that is, books are based on profit potential. In independent presses, especially progressive presses, decisions to print are topic-based or based on literary merit, that is, books are mission-driven or have something to say." (Anderson, "The Other 90 Percent," 12)

"Self-published materials allow us to reach other sectors of our customer base. Some zinesters' self-exploration will appeal to young adults. The serendipity of discovering something different will cause others to pick them up. Zines provide community networking and news. They provide entertainment and information. They educate and enlighten." (Zobel, "Zines in Public Libraries," 6)

"The value of alternative publications lies surely in their providing interpretations of the world which we might not otherwise see and information about the world we simply will not find anywhere else." (Atton, "Beyond the Mainstream," 60)

And a Different Perspective

"The Library Bill of Rights overgeneralizes. To consider 'all people' as target patrons constitutes a large, if not impossible, audience to satisfy. If a community shows no interest in authors of a particular background and viewpoint, a library wastes its resources in purchasing materials no one reads . . . The Library Bill of Rights promises too much by requiring material reflecting 'all points of view.' Library patrons may lack interest in 'all points of view' even if resources for all viewpoints were available." (Gordon B. Baldwin, "The Library Bill of Rights—A Critique," *Library Trends* 45, no. 2 [summer 1996]: 20)

Why Collect Zines?

While zines comprise only a small part of the vast alternative press spectrum, they are the most overlooked part, especially by libraries, on account of their ephemeral nature, unorganized distribution, and erratic publishing schedules. Perhaps even more important factors are the relative obscurity in which zine culture flourishes and the inherent difficulties associated with acquiring zines, especially for a formal library collection. The extra work involved is what keeps most libraries from adding a substantial amount of alternative press materials to their collections, and this is compounded when dealing with zines.

The alternative press in general operates under similar, if distinct, conditions, but librarians have little trouble expanding into alternative materials once they know where to look (and assuming they can arrange the priorities, time, and money to accommodate the new direction). Zines, on the other hand, represent new territory for the majority of librarians, and even those familiar with zines and zine culture may find integrating them into the library a daunting task. It would be disingenuous to suggest that there are not fairly impressive roadblocks which hinder, if not squelch altogether, most attempts to collect zines, but despite these inherent difficulties, zines do have a place in the public library alongside the rest of the alternative and mainstream press. In addition to the (I hope) compelling philosophical arguments discussed in chapter 3, there are a number of other excellent and specific reasons to include zines in library collections.

Zines: Join the Conversation

Zines add depth and scope to library collections, offering patrons a diversity of style, content, and subject matter unparalleled elsewhere. Strong collections are built through diversity, and zines offer information and viewpoints which no other form can duplicate. Moreover, zines are personal—without the filters of publishers, editors, and critics—and many patrons crave the unprocessed experience they offer. Reading a zine is like peeking into someone's life (even if the subject of the zine isn't expressly personal) and that connection is a big part of their appeal. (And the fascination that connection holds should be pretty obvious, what with the wild popularity of chat rooms, reality television shows, and the like.)

While the same sort of general statement about glimpsing someone else's life could be made about most artistic endeavors, zines offer readers an unequaled forum for participation; not only is there the possibility of contributing to the conversation through one's own zine, but in some sense there is the expectation that the reader will do so. Anyone can make a zine, and they needn't depend on anyone but themselves in order to make it happen. The result is a sort of hyper-democratic, ultra-creative, highly inclusive conversation that you'll not find elsewhere—at least not in print—that directly reflects the lives of its participants. It's possible to document, preserve, and share this singular conversation, and since the manner of communication and the subjects discussed speak directly to a wide variety of patrons, isn't that reason enough for librarians to investigate?

Mission: Attract and Serve Alienated Patrons

Let's talk about those patrons for a moment. The way I see it, there are two kinds of patrons out there: those who use the library and those who don't, and we need to serve them both. We serve *library users* best by providing the materials and services they need, when and how they need them. Sometimes this means helping them formulate and define those needs, and sometimes it means using our expertise to offer materials and services that we feel can address a perceived need. In any case, library users are patrons familiar with, at least to some extent, the library and what it offers them.

On the other hand we have library nonusers, patrons (or more accurately, potential patrons) who for some reason or another do not use the library. They don't visit it, don't use it, perhaps don't even think of it; the library is not an institution or an idea that resonates with them. Shocking, I know. I can't imagine life without libraries—above and beyond working in them, I can't imagine how I would live from day to day without the information, access, materials, and services they provide. But believe it or not, there are people out there for whom the library does not, for all intents and purposes, exist. It wouldn't occur to these people to call the library for information about something, to hold a meeting or study group there, to look to the library for entertainment. Why? It's certainly not a question of intelligence or education or culture, each of which I could refute as factors, given time and space. Past experience, upbringing, and the place of the library among friends and family and community could all be contributing factors, though I imagine there are numerous reasons why some people evolve into library nonusers. But this is not the place to examine that question closely, because the answer may not really matter in the long run.

What really matters is that we as librarians actively and preemptively reach out to these patrons, in whatever way that works, and turn them into library users. I've found it helpful to think of myself as a drug dealer, or alternatively as a missionary: my job is to spread the word, to hook people, to get them invested in a new way of life. I believe in the library as an idea and as a physical institution. This belief translates into a sincere desire—shared, I assume, by other librarians—to spread the word, pass on the library addiction, convert nonusers, and share the wonder. Preaching the message of libraries, what they represent, what they mean, what they empower us to be, is becoming increasingly important, both for the survival of the library, and—again, at the risk of being melodramatic—for the survival of society, making our proselytization essential. Besides, you wouldn't want to consign innocent patrons to a life without libraries, would you? Of course not.

So let's look a little closer now. We've established that there are many people who for one reason or another do not patronize the library. Some just don't think of the library at all; others when they think of it do so in a negative light. Many members of the library nonusers group feel marginalized, alienated from mainstream culture, for whatever reason. Among the groups frequently identified as being estranged from the mainstream are feminists, environmentalists, survivalists, fundamentalists, anarchists, libertarians, monastics, socialists—any of the -ists or –ians, really—racial minorities, gays and lesbians, homeschoolers, the poor, the homeless. Teens, with their long-standing tradition of alienation, are another underserved group. For many of these people, a library is simply a government institution which, when it comes to mind at all, seems to have no relation to their interests, needs, or circumstances. This is not to say that current library collections and services might not include precisely what library nonusers need, were they to investigate. In some cases it really is just a matter of publicity. However, if collections do not offer a wide variety of viewpoints, topics, media, and styles, library nonusers just might be right in thinking they will not find what they're after at the library.

When it comes to creating strong, diverse collections that aim to serve the needs of *all* patrons—users and nonusers alike—zines offer something not found anywhere else, something absolutely unique. Patrons who, for whatever reason, found nothing (or thought they would find nothing) of interest to them are astonished to find zines in the library, either because they didn't know zines existed, or because they did, but never expected to find them there. Zines offer patrons something completely unexpected, which has the benefit of getting patrons' attention, keeping it, and broadening their view of what a library might offer.

Zines also inspire nontraditional programming, which gives librarians new opportunities to share not only the zines themselves but also what they as librarians know and can offer, opening previously uninterested minds to the possibilities of libraries. Zines can truly engage alienated or disenfranchised groups—including the ever-coveted teen population—in a way nothing else can, because they speak directly to individuals and because their mere presence helps chip away at the conventional image of libraries. Zines offer patrons the physical embodiment of some of our most esteemed values, proof that the underlying philosophy of libraries is perhaps much different than they might have supposed. For example, teens, I believe, just want to be treated like real people, to have their opinions count, their experience validated. They want to connect with other people. Zines do that by offering teens a venue where anyone can play, sort of an open mike situation where all they have to do is step up and make their voice heard. Libraries can contribute in the same way by ensuring equal access to information, by treating teens with the same respect they do other groups, and by offering materials and services which speak directly to their needs. The core ideas—personal empowerment, the validity of individual experience, the equality of participants—are the same.

While this similarity of ideas seems self-evident to me (and I hope, to you), to a library nonuser it is definitely not. The first time I attended the Underground Publishing Conference (now the Allied Media Conference) at Bowling Green University, I arrived feeling confident that others would see the obvious (for lack of a better word) synergy of zines and libraries and would welcome the news of a substantial collection in a large urban library. Wow, was I wrong. Now there were definitely people thinking on the same wavelength as me, but I was shocked at the amount of negative feedback, the suspicion, the downright hostility my announcement met with in the beginning. I honestly had no idea that thoughtful people saw libraries as at best irrelevant and at worst as an enemy, and yet so many of those incredibly bright, articulate, creative people held libraries in contempt. Why?

They gave various reasons: some amount of suspicion is leveled automatically at any government institution; libraries perpetuate media conglomeration by collecting and supporting mainstream publishing; libraries censor their materials or at least bow to censorship by vocal minorities; libraries don't respect privacy, offering records and personal information to authorities without a fight, etc. Rather than sharing details of the new zine collection at my library, Brooke and I spent the weekend explaining, defending, and describing the realities of library values, beliefs, and practices. Once we had discussed things like free and equal access to information, "The Freedom to Read" statement, and the principles upheld by the *Library Bill of Rights,* and once we had corrected a couple of scarily inaccurate stories (mostly about libraries turning over records or discarding controversial materials), the conference attendees began to see our collection (and libraries in general) in an entirely different light. And once they understood that we really were collecting zines—the real thing, not some watered-down version—it was their turn to be shocked, in a good way, as they realized how cool libraries could be and how truly our values meshed.

On that occasion, as on many others to come, zines were the foot in the door, so to speak, which allowed us to educate and enlighten library nonusers about libraries. We captured their attention by talking about zines—a subject either near and dear to them, or new and exciting—and used the resulting conversations to slip in a little library advocacy and education. Alternately, we can take experienced and savvy library users and introduce them to the fascinating world of zines, where they may find just what they're looking for, whether they knew it or not.

And zines *can* be the answer patrons are looking for. Here's an example: I'd attempted to help a fairly distraught mother whose teenage daughter was cutting herself. On at least two previous occasions this poor woman had come to the library seeking information, solace, understanding. Help, mostly. She wanted material for herself as well as for her daughter, and I searched pretty exhaustively for both fiction and nonfiction to fill her need. The third time she visited the Teen Department she was almost in tears. None of the books I had given her was really helping. Her daughter couldn't explain what she was going through, how she was feeling, and the mother couldn't understand it. Desperate by this point, I dug up a couple of zines that I knew dealt with self-injury. Two were written by young women just recently recovered, and one by a younger teen who was still cutting but was trying to help herself quit by writing about it. A week later the woman was back, and this time she really did cry. Where fictional accounts, professional analysis, and self-help suggestions had failed, those zines had succeeded. Not only were they exactly the sort of connection the daughter had been craving, but she had started corresponding with all three authors and had, in essence, created her own small support group. At the same time, feeling more secure and less "freakish" allowed the daughter the freedom to seek help, both from her mother and from professionals.

I have to say, I was pretty moved. If I ever doubted that zines could serve, for some people, as a lifeline during troubled times, as inspiration when it's most needed, as comfort and support when you're all alone, I never will again. Imagine what you were like in high school. Now imagine being able to connect—without the expectations and assumptions that come with face-to-face contact—with people whose experiences either matched your own or allowed you to see them in a new way. What if you (or if you had an idyllic and fantastic experience in high school, someone less fortunate) had been able to connect with people who were also marginalized in some way. Of course, it's not just about high school; it's not as if that yearning for connection goes away after you graduate. And though with the Internet it is undeniably easier these days to find like-minded people, it's not quite the same thing as picking up a little magazine and finding your heart or mind there on the page.

Excellent Service through Strong Collections

Now that we've discussed some of the benefits of collecting zines, and having covered the philosophical reasons for including alternative materials in library collections in chapter 3, let's focus on the more mundane realities of collection development. There seem to be two basic views on the inclusion of alternative materials. On one side of the question are those who believe that developing collections based on the conveyed needs of the public using traditional or conventional sources and methods is not only good enough but is, in reacting to public demand, exactly what they are supposed to be doing as caring, professional librarians. They're spending taxpayers' money, after all, and have a responsibility to provide what their patrons ask for.

I doubt that those on the other side of the argument would disagree with that mandate—at least up to a point. But while both camps believe that library collections should directly serve the tastes and needs of the public, proponents of the alternative press also believe that the public often does not know the extent of the materials available to them, and thus cannot request materials that they do not know exist. Please notice that I didn't say, as I have often heard this argument stated, that the public does not know what they *need*. That's a remarkably arrogant statement and places librarians in a position of power which is unwarranted and, moreover, scary. I for one certainly did not become a librarian in order to arbitrate taste or dictate action or weigh in on the decisions individuals make about their lives. What I said is that while patrons very often know exactly what they need—though they may not know how to express that need easily—they very often do not know *what is available,* and that is where we come in. Our job is to show them what is available and then to help them select the material that best serves their needs.

Obviously I agree with this second position; it is our responsibility to seek out, acquire, and provide the widest range of materials possible to ensure that patrons have the widest range of choices. Because of our unique position, we as librarians have the opportunity and the mandate to explore deep, far, and wide to unearth helpful, intriguing, demanding, and revolutionary materials and offer them to the public. Self-censorship—or censorship by omission—has no place in a public library. While librarians are trained, and expected, to select the best publications for their collections, their view of what is the "best" is skewed if they do not include alternative publications in the selection pool. Mainstream views and publications are a very small part of the spectrum of thought, but they are given an inordinate amount of space and resources. Public libraries should aggressively acquire materials in every subject and medium available to them, within the bounds of their abilities. Hiding behind the myth of popular demand demeans our most basic service, our special position within the publishing industry, and our singular skills as librarians.

Yes, the idea that all ideas have merit, whatever form they come in, turns the established publishing/reviewing/collecting structure on its head. It makes our work as librarians infinitely more difficult as we attempt to include not just works to which we have easy, respectable, and defined access, but also works which are obscure, marginalized, or on the fringes of society. It's hard enough to do a good job selecting materials from the many sources available to us already; adding the innumerable and enigmatic offerings of the alternative press is enough to overwhelm and confuse even the best of us. These high-minded ideas may seem far removed from the day-to-day world of running a library, but that doesn't mean that we can't keep them in mind, can't put them into practice incrementally, can't slowly shift our habits and priorities until they align more honestly with what we say we do.

Building Strong Collections: Beyond Reviews

It's easy to talk about including alternative materials in libraries, but it's not nearly as easy to actually do it. I mean, where do you start? If *Library Journal* is off-limits, how do we know what to buy? (It's not, by the way, and neither are all the other excellent review journals out there. Of course we'll keep using them—

they're our access points to a great deal of material, and are a great source of information. All I'm saying is that they shouldn't be the be-all and end-all of collection development.)

The real question to me seems to be, without the authority and respectability of the established press to help limit and support our collection development practices, how do we decide what to include in our collections? And it's a completely valid question, practical and thoughtful. However, I think the question needs to be rephrased: if we as librarians do not give authority, respectability, and support to new ideas and new voices, who will? If we do not provide our patrons with access to revolutionary ideas and methods of communication, who will? While that answer does not really address the original question, I think it sets us on the path that will.

Another relevant question: why is such importance placed on the authority of professional publishing? We as librarians know better than most the amount of bad content and bad presentation that are out there for public consumption. Publishing houses often publish works which we would never consider purchasing, and review journals often print opinions that we find scandalous, or at least dead wrong. So why is it that we are afraid or unwilling to look outside these structures to find exceptional content and unique presentation?

Our dependence on the mainstream publishing industry is completely understandable. Not only do we depend on it to help narrow our choices to a manageable number—as is the case if we order only from established sources—but we also expect it to support our choices in the form of reviews, lists, features, and publicity. It's much easier to purchase a potentially controversial book with a starred review from *Booklist* than it is to include an almost certainly controversial zine which has no stamp of approval from a respected authority attached to it.

But in this case we ourselves must be the authority that advocates for inclusion. And why not? Many of us write the reviews which our colleagues base their selections on. Many of us know the editors and publishers who provide us with the materials we consider adding to our collections. What "authority" are we relying on if not our own? We as individual librarians are experts in forming collections of exceptional, unique, and useful materials—it's one of the things we do best. We just have to allow ourselves to do it.

Current Library Collection Development Policies and Guidelines

One of the first roadblocks in collecting zines and other alternative press materials—the one that can squelch the mere idea of a collection—is often a library's own collection development policy. Many material selection policies not only do not include the alternative press, but they exclude it, though perhaps not purposely, by their wording and intent. Unconvinced? Well, a typical collection development policy often includes some variation on the following statements: "select items useful to patrons," "select based on demand for the material," "select based on the reputation of the author and publisher," and "select based on popular appeal and the number and nature of requests from patrons." These should all sound familiar to you, as well as fair and reasonable.

But look at them more closely and we can see that unless the selector is highly conscious of the matter, these innocent phrases do indeed exclude the alternative press, and certainly zines, as much by what they say as by what they don't: "select items useful to patrons" (but with no discussion of who are or who *could be* our "patrons" and with no explanation of what "useful" means); "select based on demand for the material" (even though demand can be manufactured and people can't demand what they don't know exists); "select based on the reputation of the author and publisher" (often not known in the case of alternative materials, and while a helpful guideline in general, does not take into account where that "reputation" comes from and what it really means); and "select based on popular appeal and the number and nature of requests from patrons" (even though "popular appeal" is a completely subjective phrase which almost guarantees that the needs and tastes of a large segment of patrons will be overlooked).[1]

I especially like the irony of the phrase "number and nature of requests from patrons." While the most obvious interpretation is that libraries should buy what their patrons request, I wonder how we gauge the nature of requests from patrons we never see? Isn't that a request in and of itself: get something of interest to me, something relevant to my life, something I need or want. If we don't have those materials, why *would* a patron come to the library? What about the requests we never receive? How do we respond to those? Can we? Shouldn't we at least try?

How Do You Find Zines and What Do You Do with Them Once You Get Them?

But how? You're convinced and you want to begin adding zines to your library collection. How do you find them? What do you do with them once you've got them? Chapters 6, 7, and 8 concentrate specifically on the various answers to these questions, but it wouldn't be amiss to discuss some of the difficulties here first. The first practical problem in adding zines is access. As Chris Atton writes, "The problem of subject access, of getting a 'feel' for such a vast area is very problematic. Hidden from view, not advertised in the trade press, hardly ever reviewed in the 'quality' press; how do you find out what is available?"[2] In order to include zines and other alternative publications, librarians must be truly engaged in the effort and must often be willing to do a lot of extra work in seeking out and evaluating new materials and formats. Review zines and distros (discussed in more detail in chapter 6) provide decent access to a wide variety and a staggering number of publications, but the sheer volume of available titles can be overwhelming.

"Alternative publications do not have the respectability accorded even popular mainstream fiction by suppliers, bookshops, or libraries. Subject bibliographies simply do not exist in most areas. Availability must be pieced together using a variety of methods, among them directories of publishers, publishers' and distributors' catalogs, and the few indexes that can be found," continues Atton.[3] Zines are publicized by word of mouth, through e-mail and websites, and especially through old-fashioned "snail mail," and librarians must be willing and able to devote time to cultivating relationships in order to successfully access materials. Personal networking within the zine community is perhaps the most common and effective way of gathering selection information, but it definitely takes more work, and much more time, than simply highlighting reviews out of *Publishers Weekly.*

Once the materials have been acquired, librarians face a whole new set of problems. Cataloging and processing, storage, and publicity issues are all among the most troublesome ones. Since independent publications rarely have ready cataloging records (and zines pretty much never), they require extra effort to add to any library system. Zines, in fact, far from having CIP information or an ISSN, often do not even have a consistent title, page numbers, or a cover date. (Sometimes there's not even a name, address, or price.) Truly creative processing is therefore required in order to retain access to items once they are in the building. Questions of cataloging and processing are usually best answered by individual libraries, which can gauge the effectiveness of various options such as creating a single MARC record for the collection or actually creating original cataloging records for new acquisitions—a massive undertaking that may or may not be worth the effort, depending on your situation. (My experiences and current direction in this regard are detailed in chapter 8.)

Once materials are in the system, "librarians need to realize that there will be little or no demand for [them at first]. It's up to librarians to make these publications available," cautions librarian Byron Anderson in *Counterpoise*.[4] Once again the librarian is required to exercise ingenuity, both in displaying new publications and in publicizing their existence to patrons (or potential patrons). Various tactics such as subject displays, flyers, and special programming can be implemented to introduce patrons to new and unfamiliar materials, but as with everything else, it requires time, energy, and commitment.

To summarize, collecting alternative publications is important, and it's worth taking the time and effort to figure it out. I believe that public libraries should aggressively acquire alternative materials in every subject and medium available to them, since the inclusion of alternative materials is necessary in order to fulfill our mandate to provide information and materials from all viewpoints. Zines, especially, are not only important as a unique collection in and of themselves, but they can also establish a link with disenfranchised and marginal populations who think that the library has little to offer.

NOTES

1. Byron Anderson, "The Other 90 Percent: What Your MLS Didn't Teach You," *Counterpoise* 3, no. 3/4 [July/October 1999]: 12.
2. Chris Atton, "Beyond the Mainstream: Examining Alternative Sources for Stock Selection," *Library Review* 43, no. 4 [1994]: 62.
3. Atton, "Beyond the Mainstream," 62.
4. Anderson, "The Other 90 Percent," 12.

The Salt Lake City Public Library Zine Collection

five

History of the Collection

Though many of the details of the founding of the City Library zine collection have been lost in the mists of time, I will endeavor here to recount as much as Brooke and I can remember about the whys and hows of its beginnings. As mentioned in the preface, I first glimpsed the underground publishing subculture through the lens of the literary small press, which opened my eyes to both the possibilities of self-publishing and the existence of a thriving community. While I was almost exclusively involved with the literary small press at that time, I occasionally chanced upon less specific alternative publications, as well as what I would now call zines. Exploring the particular community of little magazine publishers is what prompted my interest in the philosophy behind self-publishing. Learning firsthand of the quality and uniqueness of the work led me to the desire to share the wealth, so to speak, with others.

What I really remember is that as my close to ten-year career as a small press literary editor came crashing to an ignoble end, I turned my attention to publicizing the alternative press movement through my day job as a librarian in the Periodicals Department of the Salt Lake City Public Library. At the time, the City

Library was doing a fairly good job of collecting alternative publications in all formats and media, following the spirit of both the *Library Bill of Rights* and its own resource selection policy, which encouraged selectors to look beyond the mainstream when adding to the library collection. The singular collection in the closed-stacks Periodicals Department attests to the commitment of selectors.

While the City Library's resource selection policy always affirmed support for selecting alternative press materials, early in 1997 I decided (for some reason) to ask for a small budget to add even more alternative publications to the larger periodicals collection in an attempt to document and publicize the underground literary world I had spent so much time in. Following my own advice, however, I wanted to collect not just literary magazines but all sorts of small press journals, alternative publications, and underground magazines which were, for the most part, hidden from sight. The original idea was to create an alternative press collection made up of sample copies, a few subscriptions, and reference materials which, though not necessarily offering complete runs of publications, would at least let patrons know about this unseen world that existed below the radar. Patrons would have to pursue publications of interest on their own, but at least they would know about them and would have the chance to investigate them further if they wished. (This strategy was due to the obvious inability of the City Library—and I suspect, any library—to subscribe to thousands of alternative publications; not only would the cost be astronomically prohibitive, but where in the world would we put them?)

Accordingly, I drafted a proposal which I luckily kept in my files (though sadly, reading it over has not jogged my memory, or anyone else's, so we're still trying to reconstruct those early days). The proposal very briefly discussed the broad philosophical reasons for creating a separate alternative press collection, detailed the amount of money needed to begin, and requested space and furniture for the collection, and a little time to devote to the project. I also asked for a small publicity and programming budget, and described plans for quarterly "open house"-type programs which would bring other small publishers in the community together to talk, network, share or trade their work, and discover new acquisitions in the library collection.

Clearly, it was not an elaborate (or very complete) proposal, but it did the trick and I was granted a small budget, a corner of the Periodicals Department reading room, and permission to start building a new alternative press collection. I started by ordering reference copies of necessary volumes like the quarterly *Alternative Press Index* (the one big-budget item in the proposal), the *International Directory of Little Magazines and Small Presses, Annotations: A*

Guide to the Independent Critical Press, Psychotropedia: A Guide to Publications on the Periphery, the *CLMP Directory of Literary Magazines and Presses, Alternative Publishers of Books in North America,* the *Directory of Small Press/Magazine Editors and Publishers,* and subscriptions to relevant news and review journals such as the *Alternative Press Review,* the *Small Press Review, Scavenger's Newsletter, Gila Queen's Guide to Markets, Counterpoise,* and the legendary *Factsheet Five.* (Details on each of these publications can be found in appendix A, though some of them are no longer published or have changed shape substantially.)

After accumulating what I saw as the permanent pieces of the collection, I began scouring review journals, bookstores, the Internet, and personal contacts for appropriate publications to add to the sample copy collection. I wrote publishers asking for sample copies; I bought single copies from bookstores or direct from distributors and editors; and I collected material at library conferences, science fiction and fantasy conventions, local clubs, and eventually from patrons who came in to donate their work to the collection. At the time, I pretty much accepted anything even remotely "worthwhile," as long as it didn't include any illegal or hyper-offensive material, and our semiofficial selection policy pretty much boiled down to "is it 'alternative?'" and "it can't be illegal."

So began the alternative press collection at the Salt Lake City Public Library. About six months after receiving the go-ahead, we held our first alternative press open house, an evening program where locals could peruse the collection, trade personal publications with each other (and donate or sell them to us), or just find out what all the fuss was about. We had a pretty good turnout that first night, about fifty people or so, and we felt good about the general direction the collection was headed. There was a steady stream (or a steady trickle, more accurately) of patrons who came in asking about the collection, or asking about a specific title, or offering their own work for sale or donation. My coworkers at the periodicals desk learned to answer certain questions, direct others to me, and came to either hate or love having the collection around.

But as has happened numerous times over the course of the last seven years, the more we were engaged by the collection, and the more we thought about what we were doing, and the more research we did about the alternative press and about libraries across the country, the more our attitude toward the whole thing changed. I especially began to dislike the separation between the "official" periodicals collection and the alternative press collection, which struck me as necessary (given that we would never have enough money to subscribe to all the publications in the alternative press collection—a prerequisite of being added to the main collection) but also as judgmental. It was as if we were saying, here's the stuff you know and want, and then here's this other stuff over here that's weird and "alternative" and not really ready to play with the other children. It's Other and belongs over here in the corner.

Of course, this was exactly the opposite of what we wanted for the collection. We were attempting to expose patrons to the amazing variety of alternative publications available, not set up some kind of freak-show collection which begged to be browsed but not taken entirely seriously. What we wanted to do was to place alternative publications alongside more mainstream fare and have them used and judged equally, but collecting all the alternatives in one place and labeling them as such seemed to be having the opposite effect. It was a quandary because our ability to collect depended very much on the way the collection was set up—that is, our reliance on sample copies—but that very setup was having the effect we least wanted and expected.

After much soul-searching, the reading of innumerable articles loaned from libraries across the country, and endless discussion, we decided that while decently popular, the alternative press collection was simply unmanageable in its current incarnation. What to do? Admit defeat and scrap the whole thing? Focus on one area such as fanzines or literary magazines and ignore the rest? More soul-searching and discussion resulted in the following conclusions. What we really wanted from an "alternative" collection was to (1) let patrons know that such an underground network existed, (2) make sure they knew they were invited to participate, and (3) help them to do so. What we really wanted, though I would never have put it in these terms at the beginning, was to help people understand that they had the power to join the collective conversation through self-publishing and that their contributions would be treated—and should be treated—with the same legitimacy the mainstream press enjoyed. What better way to do this than to add these publications to the collection? Who better to offer that legitimacy to than to the individual? So rather than focusing on one type of publication—fanzine, literary magazine, etc.—we decided to focus on a format—zines—which was the embodiment of all the ideals and requirements elucidated in our conversations.

We felt that by focusing on zines as a *format,* rather than on the *content* of publications, we could not only build a coherent and manageable (though I use that term loosely) collection and give legitimacy and publicity to zine publishers, but we could also legitimize the library itself by allowing—as I think the spirit of the library dictates—anyone—*anyone*—to participate in the publishing process. We would add that cacophony of voices to the institution of the library, thereby legitimizing both of us, as well as adding a unique and valuable new format to the collection. It seemed like the perfect solution at the time: once people get a glimpse of that hidden culture they rarely go back to ignoring it, and from the world of zines it is very easy to travel the path to the literary small press, to fanzines and clubs, to slick alternative magazines, and beyond. Zines would push the door open and once someone stepped through, our original mission to publicize the alternative press would have been accomplished, at least as far as we could help.

So we shifted our focus. We didn't immediately get rid of the slicker alternative publications, but waited for them to become outdated or fall into poor condition. Then we took them to our Friends of the Library book sale area to be available for the public to purchase, though we encouraged the library to permanently add the titles that had been most popular. Rather than ordering any more of that sort of thing, we added a couple of review zines which dealt exclusively with zines such as *Zine Guide, A Reader's Guide to the Underground Press,* and *Xerography Debt* and then we started ordering.

I remember right before our next open house (cleverly called "An Evening Underground" to allude to the position of the Periodicals Department in the library—in the subbasement of the building, two floors below ground level—as well as to the zines), I sent a sizeable order to Erica Bailie-Byrne at Pander Zine Distro in order to fill out the sparse collection in time for the program. (Ordering from review zines and distros is covered in chapter 6.) I think I asked her to send me one copy of every title in stock (the total was about a hundred dollars), so that we would have a bunch of cool new zines to display. While she was a little taken aback by the transaction, she was amazingly helpful and prompt, and we received our last-minute order just in time for the program, which was a resounding success. So the City Library zine collection as we know it today was born. (See figure 5.1.)

Skip Ahead Five Years . . .

Once the decision was made to focus solely on zines, a great many details fell into place. Our space was more suited to zines (though we outgrew it almost immediately), and zines definitely leant themselves much more easily to the sorts of programming and outreach we were eager to experiment with. We made lots of big plans at the time, and had lots of grandiose ideas about the future and direction of the collection—most of which, I'm happy to say, have come true, or are in the process of doing so. The collection itself has expanded immensely, and taken turns we love, but did not expect at first.

Early in 2002, members of our library system's Teen Task Force came up with the idea to add zines at our five branches and in the Teen Department at the main library. These small collections would be made up of specially selected zines, suitable for teens, and (most exciting of all) they would be available for checkout. We talked about the different possibilities and spent some time figuring out how to make the circulation work (given that the zines weren't cataloged and therefore didn't have bar codes) and then wrote up a proposal and sent it to the director. Two weeks later we were the proud parents of six new mini-collections. (See figure 5.2.) A more detailed explanation of our circulation scheme can

Figure 5.1   Alternative Press Collection in the Salt Lake City Public Library (Old Building)

Figure 5.2   Mini-Collection of Zines at a Salt Lake City Branch Library

be found in chapter 7. As mentioned, the zines in these collections were tailored for teens and we made a special effort to collect titles produced by teens themselves. For general-interest zines we began ordering seven copies at a time, rather than one, which I have to say really freaked out most zinesters—in a good way.

The main zine collection, up until now, has been set apart from the rest of the library materials both physically and by exclusion from the library database—again by necessity rather than philosophy. (See chapter 8 for a detailed discussion of the history of the collection's separation from the rest of the library, and more important, its recent integration!) But its very presence in the library makes the statement we intended all along, and serves as an open invitation for patrons to explore the world of the alternative press and then join, if they so choose, the conversation on their own terms.

Description: A Picture's Worth a Thousand Words

As you can see from figure 5.1, the old zine collection was a bit messy, to be kind, and a bit unorganized, to be downright blunt. The zines were displayed face out (a blessing we did not properly appreciate at the time) in old magazine racks scavenged from the basement, and though they were often layered several zines thick due to lack of space, patrons had a fairly easy time browsing the collection. A nearby table held the reference books and subscription copies, and was available to hold flyers and other freebies which zinesters often included with our orders (or which locals brought in for distribution). I still think it looked pretty cool. The trouble was that there was no order to the thing, and no access whatsoever. New zines were added, and really old ones (or multiple copies of the same title and issue) were taken to the back room and deposited in a box at my desk. (The theory was that patrons could ask to see them if needed, though of course this never happened since no one but us knew they were there.) It was most definitely a browsing collection. Still, it worked for the time and place, and in some ways I miss the cool, scattered, haphazard feeling of that space.

It's not that we didn't love the space we had, but once we heard about the proposal for a bond issue to build a new main library, our minds started working and our imaginations went crazy. We knew that the collection had received enough attention from local media to warrant a space of its own in the new building, and we were pretty sure we'd get the opportunity to at least venture opinions about what that space should look like.

We discussed fantasy shelving configurations, how much room we thought we needed, and the type of displays we were dying to create. From the beginning we had a good idea of where the collection would live in the new building—it would stay on the same floor as Brooke and I, which, conveniently, would house the magazines and newspapers, the Teen Department where Brooke and I were to work, and the Fiction Department. We thought it an ideal location, and so it has proven to be. As far as placement on the floor itself, we were offered a perfect and lovely section of shelves at one end of the magazine section—and offered twice as much space as we had planned to ask for! Of course we jumped at the chance to take over such a large piece of real estate, and our plans for the collection expanded exponentially.

By that time we had begun the enormous task of adding all the zines in the collection to an Access database created for us by a technically proficient colleague, Robyn Masters, and were using that database to track orders and produce lists of holdings. After much discussion (recounted in excruciating detail in chapter 8), we came up with a list of subject headings which we assigned using the database, and we were able to run lists of zines by title, acquisition date, and subject. The idea was to keep a paper copy of these lists out on the table with the reference materials so that patrons would at least know what we had (though it was still up to them to search the racks for specific items). So we figured we would shelve the zines by subject in the new building, and Brooke began entering in the thousands of zines we had acquired before we started using the Access database in order to have the collection ready by the February 2003 opening of the new building.

The only drawback was that we would be using the same sort of shelving as the rest of the magazine collection, with a few variations which I'll discuss in a moment. Not that we had come up with any better alternatives, but we were uncertain how the zine collection would fit into the space, given the drastic differences between zines and magazines (size being one of the main issues), and given that we wanted to sort them by subject. We asked for some flat shelves in addition to the slanted display shelves, as well as some bars from which to hang bags. We planned to put especially fragile zines, zines with many pieces and parts, and intricate zines in the kind of sturdy bags traditionally used for children's book and tape kits—it was to be our "special collections" area and we hoped the heavy-duty bags would protect the zines and keep all the parts together while displaying them nicely.

We also put in a proposal to the director to purchase comic book covers and backing boards for each zine in the collection. We hoped that by covering the zines we could unify the size a bit, protect them, and give ourselves a different surface to put labels on (such as subject and title), since many of the zines were so small that there was no room on them unless you covered actual content. We purchased two sizes of comic book covers and boards in bulk, as well as labels which we could print using the Access database. Just covering the zines took hours upon hours, but it has made a world of difference in the appearance of the collection, and in the longevity of the zines.

Once we were able to get into the new building and see the actual physical space and the shelves we were to inhabit, it became clear that we would need to make a few adjustments and that we had some new complications to think about. We were determined to have the bulk of the collection—if not the whole thing—out there on the floor for public use, which meant no more face-out display; there simply wasn't room. By this time the collection had grown to over 5,000 zines and there was just no way we could shelve them as we had done in the past. So we rearranged a little, shuffled things around a bit, and, finally, in February 2003 moved into our new digs.

As you can see from figures 5.3, 5.4, and 5.5, we now have the zines in comic book covers, shelved in rough alphabetical order (by title) on flat shelves with dividers to keep them more or less upright. We do have considerable face-out display space, and the hanging bags have been a great success, serving the exact function we had hoped they would. Reference materials are housed on flat

Figure 5.3   Zine Collection in the Salt Lake City Public
Library's New Building

Figure 5.4 Shelving and Display of Zine Collection

Figure 5.5 Hanging Bags for Multipart Zines

shelves at the ends of the stack, and there's even a little room left over for flyer space. The location itself is also ideal; it's secluded but not obscure, offering a bit of privacy, but also comfort. The zines are together as a collection at the end of the magazines section, which places them as part of the real library collection, but sets them apart just a little as something unique and special.

More details about the organization of the collection are offered in later chapters (especially chapter 8), but as of now, that's a pretty concise view of what the collection itself looks like. As for specifics, as of January 2004 the collection included about 7,000 zines, about 15 subscriptions, and 20 or so reference volumes, including how-to books, academic works, popular histories, directories, and anthologies. (See appendix A for specific titles and appendix H for further recommendations.) The collection is used by a wide spectrum of patrons, from teens to seniors, punks to grade-schoolers. Most, I think, are browsers who either do their own zines or would like to, though some are just cool people who enjoy reading zines. As word has spread about the collection, we also get a steady stream of out-of-state visitors—ranging from zinesters out on tour or on road trips to curious academics and former residents—who stop by to see the amazing new library and check out the zine collection. The local zine scene is expanding at a most pleasing rate, and almost every week we get contributions from local zinesters to add to our burgeoning "locals" section.

We're pretty pleased. Though it's daunting and tends to feel out of control pretty much all the time, the zine collection is simply amazing. As its reputation grows and it gets used more and more, I am constantly grateful to the administration and to my immediate supervisor for the opportunity to have been part of its founding. There really isn't anything else like it out there (a fact I hope to change), and I have seen firsthand the incredible effects it's had on people individually and collectively. Besides, it's fun to see people's faces, or hear the disbelief in their voices, when they ask: "In Salt Lake City?"

Getting Started

Are you convinced? Hopefully you're at least intrigued, so to borrow a line from my favorite television show, where do we go from here? Well, there are a number of things I've learned along the way that I think you'll find helpful when starting your own zine library. Part 2 of this book will cover all aspects of building a zine collection of your very own, from the initial proposal to ordering and payment, from processing to cataloging and shelving, from publicity to programming and outreach. Of course, you'll need to adapt my ideas to your own environment and circumstances, but the following information will get you started and heading in the right direction.

Starting a Zine Collection

"In my initial proposal I asked for $500 a year for sample copies, $250 a year for subscriptions, and $100 a year for programming, for a total of $850—an amount that seemed paltry to me in the context of the library's complete materials budget. Those figures were more or less pulled from the ether, since I secretly had no idea how much was needed—don't tell my director that—but I guessed I would spend about two or three dollars on average per zine, so if I wanted to collect a couple of hundred zines a year I would need about $500. The subscription budget seems high in comparison, but the bulk of it (at least $200 a year) went toward the *Alternative Press Index,* with the rest for news and review publications. I planned initially on holding four programs a year and figured in twenty-five dollars per program for things like coffee and snacks. I also asked for space in the Periodicals Department reading room and permission to raid the library basement and scavenge for display racks and a table. Finally, I asked for time to work on the collection, and for the blessing of the administration and my supervisor to put it all together." (Julie Bartel, *Public Libraries* 42, no. 4 [July-August 2003]: 235)

Steps in the Process

It is possible to put a zine collection together without monetary support (in fact, it happens all the time, since many zinesters kindly donate zines to permanent collections), but it would be difficult to maintain a collection without administrative support, which is reason enough to send a formal proposal to the powers that be. You know best how things work at your institution, so you'll want to tailor your proposal to fit the guidelines, personalities, and limitations involved. Whatever the style or request, though, you'll want to address the two requirements common to any collection: you need zines, and you need a place to put them.

In order to get zines you'll most likely want to ask for money. When asking for money it's a good idea to give a context and some compelling reasons for your request, so include a paragraph or two (or more as the situation warrants) about zines—what they are, why they are important, how they will benefit patrons and by extension the library. It's likely that no one will know what you're talking about, so be prepared to share your vision and answer follow-up questions (or better yet, try and address the questions or objections you can foresee in the proposal itself). I found it extremely helpful to use quotes from ALA documents like the *Library Bill of Rights* and from my library's own resource selection policy to bolster my request.

After you've convinced the powers that be with your persuasive arguments, ask them for money. Look carefully at how much you'll need and pay attention to the hidden details. First, you'll need money for the zines themselves. Zines, on average, cost between one and three dollars apiece, so figure out how many you want, how many you can house, and come up with a total. Many zinesters are willing to donate their work, but if we value that work enough to add it to the library collection, it seems to me we value it enough to pay for it. So ask for a budget to cover costs (see the "Acquisitions" section below for detailed information on postage costs and payment issues which might affect your request).

Figure out how you are going to process the zines (discussed in more detail in chapter 7) and add in any extra costs like comic book covers, labels, security tags, etc. Do you have space and appropriate shelving? If not, decide what you need (look through catalogs from library equipment companies like Brodart or Highsmith for ideas) and add those items to your request. Will you need a separate chunk of money for publicity or programming? What kind of outreach do you envision yourself doing and what will it cost? It's not easy to come up with that first total (or at least it wasn't for me), but putting together the proposal was an excellent way for me to carefully think through what I was doing, how I was doing it, and why, so take your time and use the proposal stage to get all your ducks in a row, so to speak.

Material Selection Policies Are Your Friend

As I've alluded to throughout part 1, zines are probably not good reading matter for the faint of heart. They're honest and raw, and include language and subjects and graphics that many will find offensive. (Not all zines contain potentially offensive content, but enough of them do to warrant a strong warning.) Truly, zines offer something for everyone, but they offer something to offend everyone as well. You need to know this going in so that you are prepared for the response you will probably get to your new acquisitions. It is possible to temper the nature of your collection (witness our teen collections) but it takes extra vigilance. And you have to realize that even the most innocuous zines, even those created by teens (especially some created by teens), will probably include some profanity and some subjects that many patrons will find controversial. Therefore, it's good to address the nature of zines up front. Discuss their potentially controversial content in your proposal. Use your library's material selection policy as an added guideline and look closely at whether it will protect you or put you at odds with your institution. If your library includes the *Library Bill of Rights* and "The Freedom to Read" statement in the policy, that's a good indication that they should (should, not will) support you.

Another aspect of zines that might cause trouble for you, and which you'll want to use your material selection policy to address (I'm assuming that you all have excellent policies), is format. In my library system, the Resource Selection Policy explicitly states that we do not judge material based on format. So just because a zine is small and not professionally produced doesn't mean it's not worth our while to collect. Zines are a format and must be judged against each other, rather than against other formats. Quoting relevant bits from your selection policy should help you address, discuss, and resolve arguments like this before they start, which is an excellent tactic to use when writing up a proposal.

Acquisitions: Where Do Zines Come From?

Before you start ordering, think about how you want to structure the collection. Will you subscribe to a smaller number of carefully selected zines or will you rely on single issues? What happens if you find a zine you absolutely love? How many zines can you handle in your space? You can change and adapt as the collection grows, of course, but it's smart to start out with an idea of what you want the collection to look like. My personal opinion is that for most collections, the sheer number of zines out there argues for a collection of sample copies rather than subscriptions—I mean, why limit yourself? But I can also imagine situations—a collection specifically for teens, for example—where a smaller number of select subscriptions would work just as well, since content will be an issue and there might not be time or money to be continually adding new unknown titles. (I use the term "subscription" loosely, though; many zinesters do not offer subscriptions per se, though they will notify you when a new issue comes out. So by "subscription" I just mean that you'll keep acquiring the same title over a period of time, which does not necessarily mean you'll only have to place one order.) At the City Library we order zines of every type, covering every subject, from countries all over the world for our main collection, and I think the single-copy approach has served us quite well. We've taken the same approach with the teen collections, mostly because we can—at this point we have a fair idea of which titles will be appropriate and which titles will probably get us in trouble.

We order from a wide variety of sources, and use a number of different tactics to find and pay for zines. Depending on your approach you'll want to investigate some, if not all, of the outlets mentioned below and find what works best for you. You may also be able to find zines locally, depending on the size and character of your community, but chances are that you'll need to order a good portion of your collection from review zines, distros, or individual zinesters. So, let's talk details . . .

REVIEW ZINES

Review zines (see appendix C for contact information) are basically zines which primarily or exclusively review other zines, and they are invaluable for librarians.

Brooke and I use *Xerography Debt* and *A Reader's Guide to the Underground Press* (see figure 6.1) as collection development tools in the same way I use *Booklist*, *Kirkus Reviews*, and *Library Journal* to select books for the Teen Department. (I feel compelled to interject a brief plug for Brooke's own witty and insightful reviews in *Xerography Debt* here, which are both excellent reading in and of themselves and unfailingly helpful when it comes to ordering.)

Anyway, like their mainstream counterparts, review zines publish on a fairly dependable schedule, coming out regularly and more or less frequently, though they are occasionally delayed when Real Life interferes. (It's good to keep in mind, since you'll come to rely on them heavily, that though review zine editors spend enough hours to make it seem otherwise, publishing their zine is almost certainly not their primary occupation, so allowances must be made.) Reviews are contributed by a number of different reviewers, mostly regulars, making it easy to get a feel for the differences in style and preference among personalities. While the length and depth of reviews vary, each should include contact information, cost, and payment terms for the zine in question, as well as a website and an e-mail address if available. The bottom line: review zines are indispensable. Find them, read them, love them.

Figure 6.1   Review Zines

DISTROS

> "Distro is short for distribution. Distros are people who sell a variety of
> different zines by other people. Distros are a great way to buy a bunch
> of different zines in one place and also a great way for you to get your
> zines out to a larger group of people. There are many distros all over the
> world that focus on many different subjects and areas of interest. New
> distros are forming all the time and others are closing so they are diffi-
> cult to keep track of." (Alex Wrekk, *Stolen Sharpie Revolution,* 59)

Distros (see appendix D for contact information) are independent distribution centers, usually operated by an individual or a small collective, and are an
excellent source for zines (as well as interesting enterprises in and of themselves). While some distro owners offer a dizzying selection of zines on all subjects, many distros concentrate on a distinct type of content such as political or
anarchist zines, grrl zines, perzines (personal zines), or literary zines. It's easy to
become acquainted with which distros carry which sorts of titles, and most distros are up front about their preferences and biases. In addition to zines, distros
(havens of DIY creativity and productivity) often carry a wide array of products
such as stickers, buttons, patches, clothing, jewelry, music, and more. I mention
this primarily as a warning to the shoppers among you—distros offer unique
and wonderful creations and can be dangerous if you don't watch out.

Due to the large number of titles they offer, distros are the perfect place to
spend a lot of money at once, making them ideal for busy librarians who haven't
the time to send out numerous individual orders. After all, when you have hundreds of dollars to spend on sample copies, and you have to write a letter and cut
a check (or gather cash) for each two-dollar zine, spending fifty dollars in one
shot at a distro is a lifesaver. (More about this aspect of collecting zines in the
next section.) Making ordering even easier, most distros nowadays have online
catalogs—though there are still some good ones that are paper only—and offer
at least a couple of different payment options, including electronic payment systems like Pay Pal.

A good distro includes reviews of every zine it has in stock, as well as ordering instructions and postage calculations. A great distro is updated frequently
(so that availability notes are accurate) and includes cover scans of each zine,
comments from readers, and quotes from other review sources. Distros do occasionally close or go on hiatus—sometimes without much warning—and since
they are often run as a side enterprise, service can be slow. But the majority of
distros, especially those that have been around awhile, will dazzle you with their
inventory, efficiency, and helpfulness.

WORD OF MOUTH

A final but no less necessary source for zines is simply "word of mouth." By this I mean zines found by networking, either in person or online, with the zine community, both locally and on a wider geographical scale. It's important that you be familiar with the underground or alternative community in your area, and patrons (or potential patrons) are an invaluable source of information—both on what they want and on what they do themselves. Look for events with similar appeal in your local alternative newspaper, attend an art show or concert, check out coffee shops or independent bookstores. If your community or neighborhood has one, contact the local art space or concert venue and see if they already have zines there (many do). Usually kids in the local alternative music or art scene will at least know what you're talking about, and might just be a great deal of help. (See chapter 2 for my complete argument against stereotyping. And then go look for them anyway since they, in all their typecast glory, are a key to finding zines in your area. Unless of course you yourself are one of those cool kids, in which case you're ahead of the curve.) Connecting with even one local zinester can lead to numerous introductions and referrals, and once the word gets out that you're building a collection, they'll come to you.

Now that our local patrons know about us, we often have people who drop by hoping to show us (and sell us) their newest creation. If they can catch Brooke or me we'll take whatever they give us; usually we get their contact info and payment preferences and offer to send them a check as soon as possible. In some special cases we pay them cash from our own wallets; when that happens, we write up a quick receipt and ask them to sign it so we can send it to the business office for reimbursement. Occasionally someone will stop by and leave zines for us with payment information. More often they just donate the copies and expect no payment (though if possible we usually send them something in the mail later, whether or not they ask for or expect it).

While part 3 of this book delves more deeply into the electronic zine community, it's necessary to mention here that the Internet is going to be one of the best places to network, find zines, and get the word out about your own collection. Electronic chat lists (see chapter 11) such as the zinesters list or zinegeeks (both hosted by Yahoo! Groups) regularly include "shameless plugs" for recently completed zines, giving you immediate access to new material, as well as easy contact with the zinester in question. Chat lists also help you keep in touch with zine community politics, events, and discussions, which is important. There's even a new chat list just for zine librarians, set up by Jenna Freedman, coordinator of reference services at Barnard College; the conversations there are literally priceless. Be aware, however, that discussion on these lists is usually frank, to say the least, and no topic is clearly off-limits. The discourse is political, charged, and quite often heated, and the language is what you might expect from zinesters. Anything and everything is discussed in detail, with examples and references, and while arguments are common, the general quality of the exchanges and the information gained usually make up for the annoyance. Most of the chat lists I subscribe to are fairly high-traffic lists, with topics ranging from zines to politics to lifestyle to pop culture. It's incredibly easy to get sucked in to the discussions—these are amazing, intelligent, creative people, after all—and depending on the level of involvement you feel comfortable with, you can participate as you have time and see fit. In any case, I'd recommend joining one or two chat lists to get a feel for things—you can pay attention to the announcements and ignore the rest if you don't find it helpful or intriguing.

While we're discussing the wider zine scene, it's worth noting in closing that zine fairs and conferences (discussed in chapter 10 and listed in appendix E) are another excellent place to buy zines. Like distros, they can be a convenient way to spend lots of money in one place, and you get the added and unusual bonus of actually looking at the material you're purchasing and speaking with the creators about their work. Brooke and I try to attend one such event each year, preferably in June (the end of our fiscal year), so that we can take whatever is left in our materials budget and spend it in one fun weekend—that way we never have money left over and we prove that we can actually use all of the money we ask for (which, as noted below, was an unexpected problem).

Stamps, Cash, and Pseudonyms: How to Pay for Your Zines

Okay, you've found a zine (or zines) that you want to order—what happens now? Figuring out how to pay for your zines is the next step, and you'll need to be creative and flexible in order to find a system that works for your library, within the confines of the zine world. There are a number of accepted forms of payment within the zine community, though the overwhelming preference is for "well-concealed cash." Stamps, trades, money orders, electronic payments, and sometimes even checks are acceptable forms of payment. But don't even think— at least not at first—about invoicing; you'll need to pay up front unless you have a personal relationship with the zinester or distro you're ordering from. So let's go over the options.

Cash is the most common form of payment and by far the most preferred. In fact, zine publishers often can't accept any other form of payment, not having the means to cash checks (even ones made out to the correct name) and not being able to deal with the repercussions of insufficient funds. You may be hesitant to send cash through the mail, but it is the accepted method of payment in the zine community; we, at least, have never had a problem. It took us a while to figure out a system that the administration, the business office, and the librarians could agree on, but once we did, the ability to send cash made a huge difference in ordering. (Our payment scheme is detailed at the end of this section.) Since zine prices generally fall between fifty cents and a couple dollars, sending cash is a great option if your institution can handle it.

In many institutions, however, there is just no substitute for writing a check to pay for new acquisitions. Checks are used both as a method of payment and as a tracking and accounting system, and if your institution requires them, there are ways to make them work (though they do present unique difficulties). The first problem: not all zine listings include a full (or even a real) name, making it difficult to ascertain who to make a check out to. The second problem: many zinesters, whether you know their name or not, do not accept checks, period. We've contacted zinesters by letter or e-mail, explained our situation, and received permission to send a check (especially if it's for more than two or three dollars), but it's a time-consuming process and doesn't circumvent all of the problems. In almost every case, checks should be made out to the individual, rather than the zine title, and sometimes coming up with a real name is more difficult than one might suppose. Sending a check to an individual may also be against your library's accounting practices, or create other bookkeeping problems, many of which you may not even be aware of until you ask (we weren't). You'll want to get the kinks out and discover any hidden problems before you start ordering (believe me), so do some research before deciding whether checks will work for you and your institution. In any case, unless you contact the zinesters first and obtain their consent (and their real name), do not send a check for zines—they'll just send it right back unless they explicitly say that they won't.

If it's not possible to send cash, money orders are another good alternative to checks, provided you can spare the time to get them and your budget can cover the service charge. While money orders offer better record-keeping than cash, they present many of the same problems as checks. Zine listings will usually tell you exactly what kind of payment terms a zinester is willing to accept, and if money orders are specifically listed, you're probably safe sending one—either write in the name as best you can or leave that space blank. If they're not listed, contact the zinester and make certain they are able and willing to cash a money order, and, as always, find out the correct name to send it to.

Stamps (or IRCs—International Reply Coupons—for international orders) are often requested either in addition to, or in lieu of, cash, in order to contribute to the zine publisher's postage costs. "Send $1 and two stamps" is a common request, and those stamps are a necessary part of the payment, so don't forget them. Of course, if you add an extra dollar or two to the price of the zine, as we sometimes do, you can get away with not sending actual stamps, but if you have the means, I'd recommend just following directions. Keeping a supply of stamps on hand to add to orders is ideal, but if that's not possible, do something to address that extra cost. Make whatever you substitute for stamps worth it, since often those two stamps are probably meant for the envelope containing your order, ensuring a speedy turnaround time and one less trip to the post office for the busy zinester. If you're not sending stamps, don't just tack on the equivalent cost because that won't quite cover the inconvenience. (It's worth noting, however, that the practice of asking for stamps as part of the price seems to be fading away—it still happens, but not nearly as often as it did five or ten years ago.)

Though not really applicable to a library setting, trades are another form of payment so pervasive and so characteristic of the zine community that you should be aware of them (especially if you've become inspired and plan on creating a zine of your own). The idea is pretty basic—I'll send you my zine if you send me yours—and trades are most popular with people who want to collect zines as well as produce them. Trades are expected to be fair—you can't trade a small ten-page zine for a larger fifty-page zine, or a carefully handmade creation for a sloppy photocopied affair—but other than that, it's pretty much anything goes. You can also trade things—or trade for things—besides zines, such as mixed tapes, craft items, and other zine scene paraphernalia. Trading is fun and it's characteristic of the zine community. But sadly, not really for libraries.

HOW WE DO IT—JUST SO YOU KNOW

After much trial and error (I'm talking *years* of trial and error), we have come up with a system at the City Library that works for all of us—administrators, librarians, and zinesters. First we type up a formal letter for each order (though they tend to get progressively less formal the better we know the zinester in question; hopefully the business office doesn't read them too carefully. . .). We usually add a Post-it note to the unsealed envelope with payment directions which include the amount owed, the form of payment, and the name, if one's needed. (This not only saves the business office time, but might save us the embarrassment of having them read our silly order letters.) For orders under four dollars we are allowed to send cash; for orders over four dollars the business office cuts a check, or I purchase a money order if necessary. The business office keeps a copy of our orders (as do we) and subtracts payments from our zine budget (for which we are eternally grateful). We do the same thing with our own budgeting system, but we, of course, chose this path, whereas the business office had it thrust upon them, little imagining ten years ago that they would soon be tracking teeny-tiny expenditures sent out in minuscule amounts.

And Finally . . .

As this chapter draws to a close, I just want to add a couple of miscellaneous comments about lessons learned and practices refined along the way. First, sometimes we send more money than is requested—in fact, in many cases we just throw in an extra dollar or so, in addition to stamps or money for stamps. There are a couple of reasons for this: zinesters tend to price their zines low (at least we think so) in order to conform to acceptable zine scene standards, and if we know the price is low, we add an extra buck or two. Also, if no price is listed in a review or ad and we don't have the time to check first (if only a mailing address is given, for example), then we guess. As I said before, most zines are between one and three dollars, so we send three or four dollars and hope that covers it, rather than writing and waiting and then ordering once we hear back. As a general rule, we pay about three dollars per zine (unless they are listed for a higher price) and rarely send smaller amounts. So, round up—that extra dollar won't make a lot of difference to you, but will be greatly appreciated by the recipient who, after all, probably spent at least three to five dollars producing the zine you're ordering.

Now that I've convinced you to send money—even extra money—when ordering zines, I better tell you what actually happens (to us at least) so you'll be prepared for it up front. Here's the scenario: we find a zine we want and send out a letter, with cash, requesting a copy. Time goes by and eventually we receive our zine—along with a couple of other zines by the same person (or in some not-so-rare cases, every zine that person has ever created) and our money back. "I'm so excited to have my zine in an actual library! Please consider this a donation to your collection (your money is enclosed) and consider adding my other zines as well (also enclosed)" is a commonly expressed sentiment in return packages. After months of trying to both keep our books straight (minus two dollars, plus two dollars, etc.) and to actually spend our budget (which we of course don't want to lose), we began adding a line in our standard order letter about not sending the money back: "Enclosed please find $3 cash to cover the cost of issue

#10 of your zine. Your work is valuable and important to us, so please keep the money as payment." It wasn't something we expected, and now that we've been frank about our need to spend our money it doesn't happen as often, but it happens enough to warrant a little warning here. (Not that having trouble spending money is such a desperate problem, but if you want to spend it all it's good to know.)

A couple of extra caveats about checks that I think are important to share. It's not uncommon for checks to go uncashed, or for them to be returned— either because the zinester wants to donate their work, or because the checks are uncashable, or because the zinester is no longer at that address, etc.—and this can lead to accounting complications and general headaches for the business people at your institution. Take pity on them and follow up with uncashed checks quickly, letting them know as soon as possible whether to cancel a check or not, whether it needs to be reissued, or whether it may still be cashed and it's just taking a long time (it can take anywhere from a week to a year to receive a zine, depending on the individual zinester). Any returned checks that don't go to them directly should be dealt with immediately so they don't hate you and your pesky, time-consuming collection.

Finally, I'd like to tell an embarrassing story about myself, by way of warning you of a potential situation involving your library board or council or governing/advisory committee. I was to receive an "anniversary award" during the library's Staff Development Day, an annual training day which included recognition of staff who had worked a certain number of years—five years, ten years, and so on. The tradition was that the library director said a few words about each recipient, phrased as clues, and then would announce the name; you'd go up, get your little gift, shake hands, and head back to your seat. The zine collection was in its third or fourth year at this point, and I knew I'd done enough time at the City Library to be up for an anniversary prize, so I was ready to hear some cute anecdote which my supervisor had shared with the director for the occasion.

Instead, the director had her own story to tell, about the zine collection and the fact that the library board had to approve each individual check *out loud* during its monthly meetings. Which meant, of course, that each month this very respectable, very intelligent group of outstanding community activists sat around and voted whether or not to accept the charge of two dollars for an issue of *Fish Piss,* or four dollars for an issue of *Fucktooth,* or two dollars for an issue of *Mr. Peebody's Soiled Trousers.* As she told the story that year, the auditorium erupted in laughter, the board members present hooted and clapped as I walked to the stage, and I turned a very interesting shade of red. I honestly had no idea that the board had to approve each check individually and *out loud*. I guess I just assumed (if I thought about it at all) that there was a list of check numbers and amounts and brief explanations and they just voted to approve that month's expenditures.

Luckily, our board is very tolerant and supportive, and obviously it was not a problem (though I'm sure at first the director was on the spot to explain the new collection and the accompanying questionable expenditures). Still, to this day when I see former board members, it is not uncommon for them to ask about a particular zine title which caught their fancy, or by which they were particularly horrified, or which stood out in some memorable way. *Blush!*

I'm not sure what the moral of this story is. But I thought you should know . . .

seven

What Do You Do with Them Once You've Got Them?

All right, you've gotten permission and some money and you've ordered a bunch of zines. How do you keep track of what you've ordered, and what do you do with the zines once they start coming in? The first thing you need (which, really, you should have in place before you start ordering) is some way of organizing your ordering system. As mentioned earlier, we began with a notebook and then graduated to an Access database and are now in the process of moving the whole operation to the library database, including our order records. As always, it depends on the size of your institution and your collection, and on what options are available and suitable. However you decide to track orders, though, you'll need to make sure the following information is readily accessible to you: what you ordered, when, from whom, how much you paid, when it arrived, and whether your order was complete. It's a good idea to keep contact information in a central location because it can be painful to try and locate it again, but be aware that it can become outdated with no notice and no forwarding service.

In most cases, zines are sent out quickly, especially if you're ordering based on an announcement of a new issue. If you're ordering from a review zine, however, the information might be outdated, despite the best efforts of the editor. Which brings us to a question that all zinesters ask: what happens if you don't receive the zine you ordered? It happens. I don't think it happens often, and usually there are extenuating circumstances such as moving, lost orders, no more copies of a specific issue, etc. Most zinesters are not out to scam you, and if you don't receive something there's probably a good explanation as to why (though you'll most likely never know what it is). If you haven't received an order after, say, two months, it's perfectly appropriate to follow up with a query. If you haven't received your order after six months you'd best just write it off, though we've had orders show up almost a year later, always with a contrite letter of explanation and apology. Sometimes you won't get exactly what you've ordered, since after selling out the first run many zinesters don't print more. In that case they'll either send a newer or older copy, or let you know if a specific distro still has copies of the particular issue you were interested in. Remember, this is a hobby (or an obsession) and not a job. Zinesters try their best, but good intentions only take you so far when Real Life intervenes, so be kind and patient and cut them a little slack. As with all things zineish, you've got to be flexible.

Processing

Once you've got a pile of zines, you'll probably need to do at least a little processing before they're ready to be put out on the shelf for your patrons. Look at how other materials are processed and decide what's appropriate for your collection. This is a tough decision—more so than it seems at first. Because zines are inexpensive, even cheap, it's easy to dismiss the need to process or catalog them—and there are completely valid arguments to be made for not doing either. In fact, when the City Library collection started, we had no intention of processing and cataloging the zines to the same standards of other library materials, for a number of reasons. First, we intended from the beginning to collect as many zines as we could, so we knew that whatever we did to them after they entered the building would be time-intensive. Second, at first there was just me and then there were only two of us, and even with the additional help of library aides and volunteers we didn't have a lot of time to devote to processing or cataloging. Third, we had a hard time, frankly, justifying the time and expense of processing and cataloging the zines. After all, they only cost a couple dollars each, and we got many of them for free, and there's no getting away from the ephemeral quality of zines in general. How could we justify elaborate processing or original cataloging? At the time, we couldn't. Besides, since we had no plans to circulate any of them and therefore they did not need bar codes, we felt we had a little leeway in how they were processed.

I'll spend much more space discussing our change of heart in the next chapter on cataloging, but as far as processing is concerned, here's a description of where we started from and what we are now moving toward. In the beginning we considered various processing options and decided to stick with what was simple, what was similar to the rest of the library and especially the Periodicals Department, and what was quick. We talked about the possibility of removing zine covers and covering them with contact paper to help them hold up better. I think we tried this with some, and while it worked well, it was time-intensive and didn't work for all zines—the ones that were more intricate or had three-dimensional parts obviously weren't well suited to having their covers removed. We settled for taping the spines to reinforce them and cover the staples, unless the zine wouldn't accommodate it. We also added a location sticker to the back of the cover that indicated the zine belonged to the Salt Lake City Public Library System, Main Library, Periodicals Department, and that it was for reference use only. Because they were relatively inexpensive, we also added "tattle tape" strips to the zines (cut to fit) for a little extra security.

As noted in chapter 5, we added circulating zine collections in each of the branches and in the Teen Department at the main library some years ago. Since the zines were not cataloged and therefore not bar coded, we had to come up with a different way of allowing them to circulate, and we found the answer by looking at other unique library collections. By following the example set by our pamphlet and map collections, we were able to circulate the zines without cataloging them. We bought boxes of large manila envelopes (specifically, grey envelopes that could be easily distinguished from others in the system) and ordered a "Salt Lake City Public Library Zine Collection" rubber stamp. We taped the sides of the envelopes so they would last longer, stamped each one to indicate that they belonged to us, and then added a bar code. As with the pamphlet and map collections, patrons could then choose zines to check out, take them to the circulation desk, and have them placed in an envelope. When scanned, the bar code would indicate that what had been checked out were zines (or pamphlets or maps, as the case may be), though there was no indication of which ones or how many. It wasn't a perfect system, but it worked well enough and allowed us to circulate the zines without cataloging them.

Then there was the matter of dots. (Good lord, the dots!) Because of the large number of magazines the City Library subscribed to, not all current subscriptions were displayed for the public in the Periodicals Department reading room in the old building. In order for the aides to easily tell which magazines went where, the reading room magazines had a small blue dot placed on the top left corner of the front cover. Since we wanted to process the zines in a similar fashion, and since we knew at some point that not all the zines would fit in the reading room, we opted for a small green dot on the cover, which told the aides (and patrons) that the item was a zine and that it belonged in the reading room. Because none of the magazines with blue dots circulated, it was also easy to convey to patrons that none of the zines with green dots circulated either. This worked well, and when a few years ago we added the circulating collections, we brought in red dots to designate zines that belonged in those collections, and more important, zines that circulated.

When we moved to the new library building we had the opportunity to look at our system again and make some changes in processing based on our new space and on the library's new security system. We were still in the process of adding the zines to our newish Access database and were quite a ways behind, since they had been accumulating for years before this new system. We wanted to get them all entered before we began our new way of processing, so that we could use the database to print new labels. Why new labels, you ask? Well, the zines had always been displayed in face-out magazine racks, in no order whatsoever, and in some ways this worked well (though in other ways—if you actually wanted to find something, for instance—it was disastrous). Shelving is discussed in more detail in the next section of this chapter, but I need to add here that after learning more about our new space and deciding what kind of shelving would be available, we figured we needed to revisit the issue. The zines would no longer be displayed face out, but would be shelved like books, upright with the spines out. Of course, most zines are quite thin, so using the spine was not really an option and we had to come up with a way to process and shelve the zines that would be helpful to patrons.

The original plan was to shelve the zines in the new building by subject (a decision discussed in intense detail in chapter 8), and we made up a label design based on that decision. The new label gave the title of the zine and the subject category under which it was shelved, and included all the other information about location and reference status mentioned above. (Since we caught up with entering the zines into the Access database only shortly before our recent change of heart, this plan was never put into action, but I still think it would work in some collections, depending on the size of the collection and the physical space.)

In order to make the new upright shelving work, however, we needed more than just labels. Zines are not uniform, and they don't stand up, and they come in many pieces and parts, and generally the idea of moving the collection as it was to the new shelving was simply unbearable. We decided to use comic book covers and backing boards to allow the zines to be shelved upright, an idea which I'm pretty sure we didn't come up with, but which has worked extremely well. (You can buy covers in different sizes, and boards that fit in them, in bulk from almost any comic book shop. If your local comic shop isn't able to help with this for some reason, or if, heaven forbid, you don't have a local comic shop, you can order them off the Internet or from catalogs.) Not only do the covers keep the zines upright, but they also protect them, keep all the parts together, and give us another surface for labels (the importance of which, again, will become clear in the next chapter). So while we didn't add subject labels to the zines before the move, we did begin placing them in the covers, and we just kept processing them as usual—taping the spine, adding location stickers, and using the dot system. Once we moved, we shelved the zines in the new building in rough alphabetical order by title, intending to rearrange them when the subject labels were ready to go. All the other processing stayed the same, except the security strip.

In preparation for a new building, the library incorporated a new RFID (radio frequency identification) security system, and had spent the year before adding Checkpoint (the company they chose) tags to every single item in the main library collection. Each tag was programmed to correspond with the item bar code, and then the tag and a cover label were placed in a specified area on the item. Because the zines had no bar code (since they didn't circulate) and because of the time involved, we never really considered Checkpointing them. Besides, the tags, while not super-expensive, were more costly than the security strips and we didn't feel able to justify the cost, not to mention the fact that the tags and covers were larger than some of the zines themselves. So we did away with the security strips and the zines were released into the wild with no tracking devices at all. I mention this little tidbit of collection trivia because in the next chapter security considerations, bar codes, and justification for Checkpointing the zine collection are discussed in depth, so it's nice to have some background. Some of the processing discussion will have to wait for chapter 8, but hopefully this short description of our methods will get you thinking about what will work within your system.

On the Shelf

Shelving

When we moved to the new building, we were able to request some specific types of shelving, though our pieces had to fit with the rest of the shelving, in that section of the floor especially, and in the rest of the library as far as the make and color were concerned. Before we made our requests we perused a number of library equipment catalogs to get ideas. We searched online for other zine collections (mostly in show spaces or alternative bookstores) to see how they did things; we especially checked out the Independent Publishing Resource Center in Portland, one of the best-organized and most impressive collections around, run by librarian Greig Means, publisher of *Zine Librarian Zine*. We asked people how they shelved their zines—by subject, title, author—and what they used—bookshelves, magazine boxes, display racks. We asked what their ideal collection would look like and how it would be arranged. We talked to zinesters online, local zinesters, other zine collection organizers, library staff, the architects, basically anyone we could pin down long enough to get an opinion out of.

We sketched out some of our ideas (some of which seem really silly and weird to me now) and showed those sketches to staff to get feedback. Then we finally got a look at what shelving style had been selected for the library as a whole, which helped narrow down our options considerably, and we began focusing on what was available to us in that style. We went back to the catalogs then, copying pages for later sketches and dreaming big. In the end we submitted our request by means of another proposal which explained our needs, the size of the collection, how fast it was growing, and what our preferences were. We requested display shelves; flat shelves with dividers for the bulk of the collection and for the reference books; hanging bags for the special collection zines; and a couple other "bells and whistles" pieces (which for the record, we didn't get). Gentry Blackburn, our resident artist and one of the original zine collection staff, drew two mock-ups of our dream shelving—one nice and serious to give to the building committee, and another very cool one which we planned to take to zine conferences and then use to publicize the big move to our patrons. (See figure 7.1 for the cool one.) What we ended up with does look amazingly similar to the request we submitted, and our excellent new space and spiffy new shelving are working quite well.

Display

How you display your zines is really a matter of preference and necessity (organization is covered in depth in chapter 8). As you pull the collection together, look at the space available and imagine what sort of shelving (if there isn't some there already) you'd like. Be creative—just about anything will work—and come up with something that fits your space, your budget, and your collection. Many zine libraries use standard bookshelves, or old milk crates, or wooden boxes, or

Figure 7.1 Artist's Mock-up of the "Ideal Zine Collection"

shoe boxes, or standard magazine boxes, or spinning racks. In a library, your collection may need to fit into whatever shelving you have already in place, and in almost every case you can make it work.

We've had to adjust to not having the entire collection face-out, but it's great to have almost everything out in the reading room for patrons to browse. Like magazines (and according to the new bookstore-style merchandising philosophy sweeping through libraries these days), it is best to have at least some face-out display space to catch attention and attract patrons. You can use actual magazine racks for this (large or small) or book stands, or just face the zines out on a flat shelf. It's nice to display new zines, or have a section for staff or patron recommendations (with those nifty comment cards like they have in bookstores). We've considered copying off reviews from review zines and attaching those to the zine in question as well—like they do in some wine stores (at least around here). Whatever you can do to attract attention and display the collection to best effect.

Both our old and new spaces had a section (a small table in the old building, a section of flat shelving in the new) where patrons (and staff) could place flyers, handouts, free stickers, and buttons. In keeping with the conversation metaphor that the zine community inspires, it's nice to have a place where people can communicate with each other about shows, concerts, readings, and other events, or publicize their zines. We offer in our order letter to distribute any flyers or free copies or trinkets that the zinester would like to include, and we regularly get packages of zines which include announcement flyers for new issues, zine fairs or conferences, compilation books, music, distros, review zines, and more. Many zinesters make buttons or stickers or patches to promote their publications, and many include a couple for us to give away in our freebie section. Local zinesters come by to leave flyers for shows or readings, to donate copies of their zine that patrons can take for free, to announce new issues or local art shows, or whatever. We also place copies of the local free alternative newspapers there.

Space

The area the collection occupies in the new building is even more ideal than it was in the old building, and for that we are very grateful. I should explain. In the old building, the Periodicals Department was in the subbasement, two floors below ground, and was sort of hidden away. If you didn't know it was there (and didn't read the signs) you'd never guess. The zine collection was kept in a corner of the Periodicals Department, which made it doubly removed from the rest of the library. While this doesn't sound like the ideal location, in many ways it was just what we needed in the beginning. The isolation allowed us to grow into something pretty impressive before many patrons took any notice. It also kept the general public away (for the most part) while we worked out all the kinks and figured out how to write up and put into practice a collection development policy. The only patrons who used the collection the first year or so were people who were really into zines and who had heard through the zine grapevine that we had a collection.

Not that I would advise this sort of setup for anyone else, and not that we didn't grumble or joke about being so squirreled away (the underground collection so far underground, etc.), but it did give us space to figure out what we were doing. And one lesson we learned from it was that many of the patrons who use the collection heavily like to do so in peace and quiet, away from others. Not that they're antisocial or anything, but zines are sort of a very social, antisocial medium, where you can join the conversation and have a voice without, if you prefer, ever really talking to people (sort of like the Internet, I guess). Anyway, many patrons commented in the old building about how nice it was to have their own space.

So, in the new building we asked for space that wasn't in the center of things, some place a little secluded or separate. We were offered the last range of shelving at the edge of the floor, next to the fireplace area (there's one on each floor)—an ideal spot. In this area we are most definitely part of the floor, but the browsing area is separated from the rest of the magazines just a little and zinesters can hang out next to the zines in relative seclusion. On the other hand, the wall they lean up against there is all glass and on the other side of it are staff offices, so there's no actual privacy, just the feeling of it. The point of this rambling description is that if possible, you should offer your patrons a little corner of their own where they can sit and read or browse the collection. Don't separate them from the library, but realize that they would probably very much appreciate having a space of their own.

Living Arrangements

eight

The Short Version

Most of this chapter will be taken up with a detailed description of the history of access to the City Library zine collection—how it's organized, why we did what we did, why we changed our minds, and where we are right now. But for those of you who either don't need or don't care about the nitty-gritty details, this section offers a condensed version, which includes only the broad questions and some very general answers. Depending on the size of your collection, various strategies might work better for you than others, and it's really best to just customize the organizational structure of your collection to your own situation. You won't necessarily need an elaborate classification system; simply sorting by subject or title or author might work just as well. But you'll need to address a couple of questions at the start in order to determine how best to proceed. The first question you'll need to answer when the time comes to organize your collection is whether you want to catalog your zines. The second question—regardless of the answer to the first question—is how you are going to give patrons access to the collection.

So let's look first at whether or not to catalog zines. On the plus side, cataloging the zines adds legitimacy to the collection, and treating them just as you would any other format makes a pleasing kind of sense. Adding them to your catalog will also allow the highest level of access to the collection (once you figure out how to do it), which is a strong argument in itself. The drawback, of course, is time. Time, resources, and know-how. I can almost guarantee that adding zines to your library database will mean original cataloging, and that takes time; as of this writing, at least, you're not going to find many MARC records—if any—to download.

Is it worth it? Can you create original records yourself? If not, are there open-minded staff at your institution with the knowledge, patience, and fortitude to do it for you? How flexible is your cataloging department? Will they allow you to set the guidelines and standards for cataloging zines? How much time will it take to catalog them? Can your institution afford to allocate staff time to the project? Is it willing to do so? Obviously cataloging presents problems.

But if you're not going to catalog zines alongside the rest of your material, how are you going to offer patrons access to them, and how are you going to arrange them on the shelf? Unless your collection is small enough to be easily browsed in its entirety, you'll really need to come up with a way for patrons to access it. If you do decide to organize in some fashion, but are not adding the zines to the database, think about how your patrons might prefer to access the collection. Will they browse by subject, search for a particular title, or look for a certain author? Unless you want to go with the "casual approach" (see figure 5.4 for a reminder), you'll need to come up with a simple shelving scheme in order for patrons to find specific items.

Subject categories can be problematic (though not impossible) to define in any classification scheme, and zines take the difficulties to a whole new level. A zine may include numerous topics in a single issue; a title may change topics completely from issue to issue; and certain categories such as "perzines" or "compilation" zines are likely to properly contain so many zines as to become unwieldy all on their own. But using title as an access point can be equally vexing, since zines quite often change titles with no warning, so trying to keep a run together can be a real headache—even more so than with a mainstream serial. More important, will your patrons know the name of the zine? My informal interviews with zinesters and City Library patrons tell me that only about half of them do; the other half know the name of the zinester. So do you shelve zines by author then? Is there any way to offer your patrons the ability to cross-reference, so that if they only know that piece of information which you have chosen not to organize by, they will still be able to find what they are looking for?

There are no right answers and, at this stage at least, not a lot of precedent to fall back on. I can tell you what we did (and do, below), but I can't tell you what will work best for your institution. The only advice I can offer is to talk to your coworkers, talk to your patrons, and ask other zine librarians about their methods and solutions. Figure out a system that works for you. Because after all, in the world of zines, it's all about innovation, creativity, and doing your own thing. If you want to know how we did it at the City Library, read on. If not, good luck.

The Painfully Detailed Version

Well, you've chosen to keep reading, so I'll assume that either you have hidden masochistic tendencies, or you're really interested in the intimate details of our cataloging history. I should say right up front that I am not, by any stretch of the imagination, a cataloger. I lack both the training (having taken only a couple of courses in library school) and the desire (though the more I delve, the more fascinated I become, I have to admit). So if my theories and philosophy are faulty, if I use certain words incorrectly, or if I just don't seem to know what I'm talking about, I hope you'll forgive me. I'm pretty much making this up from scratch, and the part where I'm not really a cataloger doesn't help, to say the least.

That said, I do think that the amount of time, energy, research, and practice we've put into the City Library zine collection is fairly extraordinary. We've worked hard to figure out how to provide access and we've learned a lot along the way. I don't know if we've solved the cataloging riddle even now, but I'm pleased with the direction we're heading in and I think we're at a point where we have insights to offer. I can at least tell you what didn't work and why, which hopefully will save you the trouble of making our mistakes. What follows is the process as I experienced it, with commentary.

Part One: As It Was . . .

ORGANIZING THE CITY LIBRARY ZINE COLLECTION

For the first five years of its existence, zines in the City Library collection lived in three tall wooden magazine racks, displayed face out, in no order whatsoever. When the collection consisted of even a hundred or so titles this arrangement—though often frustrating—worked well enough; patrons simply browsed until they found what they were looking for. This arrangement (and I use the term loosely) had more to do with necessity than choice since we simply did not have the staff, or the shelving, to put and keep the zines in any kind of order. After a couple of years, however, this system (if you can call it that) simply didn't work anymore. By that time the collection included thousands of zines, and we—patrons and staff—couldn't find anything.

I need to insert one important caveat before I continue this description, however. I'm faithfully reporting now what and how we were thinking at the time, in order to take you through our entire thought process, but I'm not going to preface every sentence with "at the time we thought. . . ." So I sincerely hope you'll read on through to the end of this chapter, since where we start is not where we end up, and opinions expressed at the beginning are not necessarily the same as opinions expressed at the end.

Right. The time had obviously come to try and bring some order to the chaos, and to do this we needed to step back and look at the collection from a fresh perspective, focusing on the characteristics pertinent to organization. So, taking a lesson from my graduate classification theory courses, and as an exercise in critical thinking, I first divided the characteristics of zines into "useful" and "not useful" information categories, and then described, mostly for my own benefit, what sort of information each category offered, what points of access gave us useful information about zines. Here's what we came up with:

Subject. Probably the most important access point is subject, though this is also the most awkward information to accurately describe. Few zines have consistent content, and few zines cover only one subject at a time. A classification based solely on general labels such as review, music, political, or perzine would not really give enough information to do the publications justice, though it might be enough of a description for a small collection. Zines do have recognized "types" that fit nicely into subject classifications, though they are not incredibly descriptive. (For example, one of my favorite zines, *Sobaka*, would probably be classified as a "political" zine even though the style and many of the shorter essays are much more "perzine." I, who am not usually interested in "political" zines, would never have picked this one up if I had thought that's all it was.) For patrons, knowing the contents of a zine is perhaps more important than any other single piece of information, so while subject is a difficult approach, it's not one that should be discounted.

Author/editor. When the author or editor of a zine is important to the user, it's *really* important. There are a number of "famous" zinesters whose names will invariably attract or repel users, depending on their tastes, and though the more anonymous zines can be highly attractive to users as well, certain authors and publishers who are well known often collect exceedingly loyal followings.

Patrons will often want to read any project—regardless of the subject or title—to which this person is attached, making this another strong contender for primary access point.

Title. The title of a zine is definitely important, as it is the "handle" patrons refer to the work by. Quite often, in fact, the only thing a potential user knows about a zine is its title, which they read in a review, or which was referred to them by a friend. Zine titles are, however, highly transitory; often fanciful; and, even more often, fairly nondescriptive of contents or style, and therefore are not in themselves a very satisfactory way of classifying a collection. For example, displaying zines in alphabetical order is a good method if the title of the zine is constant and known, or if some method of cross-referencing is available, but since this is often not the case, other access points might be more powerful.

Form. All of the elements which make up the physical form of a zine are important descriptors for the users of this collection, many of whom are interested in getting ideas of their own, or who enjoy the "art" of zines, or who want an idea of the form their work might take should they choose to send it to a compilation-style zine. Size, page length, printing style, binding, graphics, "extras," and cover material are all important elements of form. This physical description is usually indicated in zine listings by an abbreviated characterization such as "half-size/64pg/xerox/hand-sewn/photos with bonus mini and pastepaper cover." Zines do come in regular sizes, and the majority of zines can be described as full-size (8½ × 11), half-size, quarter-size, and mini (half quarter-size); this is by no means a complete list, but rather a sample of the sorts of categories that zinesters use to describe their own work. There are also many different ways, of course, to produce the physical publication, from handwritten to photocopied to offset-printed; from loose sheets folded in the middle, to staples, to hand-sewn bindings, to unusual bindings such as rings, ribbons, rubber bands, or metal prongs. Zines also often incorporate "extras" such as hidden pockets; "bonus minis" (a larger-size zine with pockets on the inside cover in which a mini zine is inserted); photographs or postcards; mini posters; or items such as stickers, patches, toys, glitter, pictures, funny advertisements, or rocks which are incorporated into the zine itself or placed in the mailing envelope as part of the "zine package." A complete physical description, while certainly not necessary, would offer patrons important information about the character of each zine.

Language. Obviously the language of a zine is important, since if you don't speak that language you can't read the zine. Bilingual zines are often of interest to those either studying a particular language or to those who are simply curious about zines from other countries. The zines in the City Library collection come from all over the United States and from countries across the globe; most are in English, some are written completely in a foreign language, and some are bilingual (either with English on one side and another language on the other, or with parts in both languages). Since language might be a barrier, alerting patrons to the language(s) a zine is written in is important.

Geographic location. Where a zine comes from, though not an essential piece of information, might well be of interest to zinesters for one reason or another. Zines from or about other countries, local zines, or zines out of certain popular cities could well be of special interest, and their geographic location will be something to note. As an access point it's not very useful, since there might be only one or two titles from any given location (unless it's one of the "hot spots" such as Portland, Boston, Toronto, San Francisco, and, for some reason, Bowling Green, Ohio, which produce exceptional numbers of zines), and it's unlikely that patrons would want to access the collection primarily through location of origin or subject, though both of those points would be nice to include in a complete descriptive scheme.

Date. Dates are important, and when known, should be included in any attempt at organization. Zines, however, often do not list a date of publication (or at least one not easily discovered), and in some respects, it doesn't matter. While patrons may need to know the date (or issue number or other chronological tag) in order to find the newest issue or a particular issue, it's not as if most zines would become outdated, given their content. Again, noting the date or issue number is helpful and important, but certainly not a primary point of access.

Cost. Users who wish to purchase copies of a zine for themselves will of course be interested in the price, but offering this information to patrons is not always as simple as it sounds. Often no price is listed on the cover of a zine, and sometimes no price is mentioned on the inside either. When a price is given, it is sometimes quite specific ("one dollar and two first-class stamps") but is sometimes quite vague ("just send what you can" or "send what you think it's worth" or "send enough for me to buy a can of soup"). Noting price where it is known is a good idea, but that information, while useful, is perhaps less important than any of the other points mentioned.

While many of the categories described above may seem fairly useless as far as organizing a collection goes, delineating them proved to be an interesting and profitable exercise (and became even more so down the road when we began looking at doing original cataloging). Given this entertaining but only mildly helpful exercise, we narrowed the list of possible primary access points down (not surprisingly) to subject, title, and author. Those of us working with the collection at the time decided that by subject was the best way to organize the zines on the shelf, since it offered patrons decent access and could be modeled after other parts of the library collection (such as nonfiction, which is organized by subject, or genre fiction, which is often separated to allow for easy browsing). It also helped us maintain a more diverse and balanced collection by allowing us to easily keep track of how many titles we had in each subject area.

CREATING SUBJECT ACCESS TO THE ZINE COLLECTION

Of course, organizing the zines by subject was much easier to discuss than it was to put into practice, and the process of creating a rudimentary classification scheme was a long and arduous one. I have to admit that at first, the idea of assigning subjects to the collection seemed time-consuming but not terribly difficult. Ha. As soon as the work actually began, it was immediately apparent that the undertaking would be a much longer process, and much harder on the brain, than I had originally thought, and so I decided to step back, do some research, and call in reinforcements. After reading various books and articles on subject access, perusing the indexes and subject guides of numerous alternative publications, and holding a number of mind-crunching meetings of the zine collection staff, I finally put together a preliminary list of possible subject headings.

I'm happy to say that very few of those original categories survived, and neither did our original one-subject-each approach. After about a minute faced with the actual collection, we realized that our initial list was not going to work and that a standardized, tiered subject classification scheme was called for. Another period of information gathering followed, and then another meeting of the zine collection staff, where we—dedicated as we are—sat at the coffee shop until we had talked through and ironed out the final subject-access classification scheme.

The scheme we finally agreed upon had two parts. First, a primary subject heading was assigned based on the majority content of the zine, which also indicated where the zine would live on the shelf. A number of secondary subject headings—up to five—were also assigned, as appropriate, and after the zine was entered into our new database, a lovely cross-referenced list was produced. A thesaurus was compiled to help patrons (and us as well) keep track of exactly what we meant by each subject heading, and it was kept with the lists for easy reference. The thesaurus contained a short description of the subject; a list, if applicable, of similar terms; and an example or two of well-known zines that fit that category. Any terms listed in the thesaurus were added to the database as well, and "see also" references were included in the final subject/title lists which were to be available for patron use.

Quite early on it was apparent that we would need to assign a hierarchical value to certain categories, in order to standardize our classification. So we invented a "trump" category designation, which meant that if a zine fit that category, that subject heading would *always* be the primary access point. This part of the classification process generated by far the most discussion, not because we disagreed, but because we had to talk our way into understanding exactly how to implement a tiered subject-access system, and then figure out which categories were the most important for our patrons.

For example, *Say Cheese* is a popular local photography zine. If it wasn't local, it would be classified first as an "Art" zine, but since we were more interested in promoting local zines than in promoting photography, it was listed under "Local," with "Art" as a secondary subject. *Muuna Takeena* provides another example. This Finnish zine is written in both Finnish and English, and contains mostly record reviews and concert descriptions. We decided that "International" and "Foreign Language" were more descriptive and meaningful labels than "Music" (a category that included way too many zines already), and used that as the primary subject. "Comics," "International," "Foreign Language," "Local," "Review," and "Special Collections" categories were our initial trump subject terms.

In practice, when a patron wanted to access the collection, they would be able to do so in a couple of different ways. Patrons wishing to browse zines on a particular subject would access the Subject List, which included a straightforward listing of each subject heading and the zines to which it had been assigned. Zines were listed under both their primary and secondary subject headings, but secondary headings were all "see" references which indicated the primary subject heading and therefore where the title lived on the shelf. The thesaurus and description of headings was included in this section so that patrons could check their terminology if they were not finding what they wanted. Patrons looking for a particular title or author could check the Title List or the Author List, and if the zine was in our collection, the list would give the location (reading room or branch) and the primary subject heading, so that patrons could find it on the shelf. Primary and secondary subject headings were listed as "see also" references so that patrons could locate similar zines as well.

This original classification system was still in its probationary period when we decided to implement grand, sweeping changes as described in the next section. But I still think that—had we not been given an extraordinary opportunity—the scheme was more or less sustainable; it was fluid, hospitable, and allowed for growth and change, all the things they teach you to look for in library school. While subject access was never ideal, and while our fairly simple scheme was never as expressive or descriptive as we might have wished, considering the material being classified, I think we did a pretty good job.

Part Two: As It Is . . .

TAKING THE PLUNGE

Late in 2003 an amazing offer was presented to us (at, I must say, an extraordinarily unfortunate time—about three weeks before the first draft of this book was due to the publisher) which changed the direction and standing of the collection to an unprecedented degree. The manager of our Technical Services Department approached us with the idea of actually adding the zines to the library database, an idea we had long ago discarded due to the seemingly insurmountable difficulties such a project would create. The most obvious problem was that neither Brooke nor I were catalogers, we didn't have access to the system or the training to create original records, and there was simply no way the catalogers had the time or inclination to take on such a project.

The manager proposed to give Brooke and me limited access to create original records, train us to do it correctly, work with us to come up with a usable standard for zine cataloging, and then let us do the work ourselves. I have to say we were actually quite shocked. We hesitated for about eight seconds, scared silly by the enormity of the task, and then we quickly took her up on her offer before she could think better of it. Of course, then we went back to our desks and debated whether or not this was really the right direction, whether the time, effort, and cost of cataloging such a large collection was warranted.

The zine collection is valuable and unique. While we very much appreciated the consideration and support we'd been given in the past, we also felt that it was time to begin treating the zines with the same attention as other materials in the system. We decided that if we (both Brooke and I, and the City Library system at large) did indeed value the zine collection as much as we said we did, we should accord it the same respect given to other formats and make it accessible to patrons through the library database. There are also other solid reasons to catalog the collection: it legitimizes both the zine collection and the library; it enables us to track statistics; and it enables us to track lost or stolen items and recoup some of the expenses. The City Library has a policy (clearly stated in the Resource Selection Policy) of not judging material by its format, and we decided that this was an excellent time to put that commitment to the test.

Besides, we had been talking ever since we moved about the possibility of circulating the entire zine collection, something patrons had been asking for in no uncertain terms, and which we felt was the proper next step in the evolution of the collection. Up to this point we had been quite reluctant to do so, however, having no way to track what was actually on the shelf, no way to replace lost copies, and no way to keep accurate statistics, so we had never really seriously considered it until this point. Being able to move from in-house use to a circulating collection was a huge bonus, and together with the immeasurably improved access that cataloging would give patrons, convinced us that this was the right thing to do.

So, after much discussion and a lot of excited planning, we decided that yes, this course of action is entirely appropriate at this point in the life of the collection, and most definitely worth the effort. We committed ourselves and began considering specifics, beginning with another proposal sent to the library director. That proposal (which was also the basis for this section) was written after even more discussion, during which we contemplated the various ways to approach the collection. We talked with both City Library staff and other librarians around the country, with zinesters and with library patrons, gathering ideas and preferences which we merged and adapted and, we think, formed into a workable approach.

In short, we decided that we would catalog the zines using books (what!) rather than serials as a model (our reasons are described below). Each zine will be assigned a unique call number, which would look like "Zine _cutter number_." The cutter number will be taken from the author's last name and then the title of the zine, as a book would be cataloged, because we feel that author is the appropriate main entry point for zines. We also decided, on the advice of a coworker, to copy our "standing order" record type, which would allow us to catalog zines individually (rather than creating one record for the title) but also to keep check-in records (masked from the public) to track orders. Our complete discussion and the conclusions we came to about cataloging are described in the next section. All of the quotes used in the section are from *Maxwell's Handbook for AACR2R* (1997) by Robert L. Maxwell and Margaret F. Maxwell, published by the American Library Association, a source we found invaluable in helping us to understand the various issues and standards in the *Anglo-American Cataloguing Rules,* 2nd ed., or *AACR2R.*[1]

ZINE CATALOGING AT THE CITY LIBRARY

The main question as we saw it was which type of record to model our cataloging after. We eventually refined this question a bit, and focused on whether to catalog the zines using a book-type record, or a serial-type record. There are benefits and drawbacks to each approach, though neither type fully captures the essence of zines, and I think valid arguments could be made both ways. Though intuitively it's a bit of a stretch, cataloging the zines like books and using the author as the main point of access make much more sense to us, and will ultimately give patrons superior access to the collection. Our discussion on this subject is recounted below.

The first question we asked ourselves when considering cataloging the zines was, what is the most important thing about zines? The second question we asked ourselves (and any patrons we saw browsing the collection) is, how would patrons prefer to access the collection *on the shelf*: by author, by title, or by subject? The answer we came to on the first question is that zines are created by one person or a small group of people and the fact that they are self-published, independent creations is probably the most important thing about them. By this reasoning it is the person behind the zine that is important, rather than the title or the subject.

The answers we received to the second question were mixed, with no one way of accessing the collection preferred. Patrons knew some titles and some authors; they liked the idea of browsing by subject, but agreed that choosing appropriate subjects would be problematic and lead to categories so broad that they would cease to be useful. Patrons and staff overwhelmingly preferred to access the collection using an online tool (like the library catalog) which would allow them to search by author, title, and subject, depending on their need.

Therefore, our preference—based on what's most important about zines and how patrons prefer to access them—is for author entry to be the main access point. This decision agrees with *AACR2R* 21.0B *Sources for determining access points*, which states that "The most important source for determining access points—in fact, the most important source for the transcription of bibliographic description—is the part of the item that may be termed 'prominent'" (*Maxwell's* 307). The author is the most prominent and consistent access point for zines and is therefore preferred as the main point of access.

Initially we planned to catalog the zines like magazines, so we thought that this preference would be a problem (since magazines are cataloged by title). However, after looking more closely at the cataloging rules, we found that *Maxwell's* offered us a loophole: "To reiterate: when choosing the main entry for a serial, the cataloger will be governed by the general principles given in AACR2R chapter 21. In order for main entry to be under the name of a person, 21.1A1 states that this person must be 'chiefly responsible for the creation of the intellectual or artistic content of a work'" (273). Zines would definitely fall under this exception.

Maxwell's further states that "because of the nature of a serial publication, entry under the name of a personal author is extremely rare. . . . As with other library materials, the content of the serial, not the name, governs the choice of main entry" (274). Zines are that rare case where entry under author name is appropriate, and the content, created in most cases by an individual, bears that out. Therefore, we were still safe in choosing author name as the point of entry, and we took this as a sign that we were on the right track as far as what is "most prominent" about zines.

So no matter what model we followed (book or serial) we would be cataloging the zines by author, since they fit into the very limited group of serials which are cataloged by author rather than title, and since the author of a zine is the most important or prominent aspect of the publication. The next questions are first, are zines really more like serials than like books? And next, which record model fits zines better? Which model is the most accommodating? Which model offers patrons the best access? Let's take each question in turn.

Are zines serials? According, again, to *Maxwell's*, "a serial, by definition, is 'a publication in any medium issued in successive parts bearing numerical or chronological designations and intended to be continued indefinitely'" (*Maxwell's* 271, quoting from *AACR2R* appendix D). While it's a stretch to say that zines offer successive chronological designations, or that they are intended to continue forever, in spirit anyway, this definition seems to more or less include zines. *Maxwell's* goes on to point out that a "serial is a state of issue, not a kind of material. Anything, print or nonprint, may be a serial, as long as it is issued in successive parts, numbered or dated in some fashion, and as long as it has no planned termination point" (271). So, as a "state of issue," a zine is sort of a serial. "'Serials constitute a type of publication rather than a condition of authorship,'" *Maxwell's* further clarifies, meaning that the fact of its being published serially and holding to the guidelines described above is what makes a serial a serial, while the author (which we have already decided is the most important aspect of a zine) is not a defining aspect (271).

At this point we needed to ascertain whether a zine is really like a serial in any way other than that many of them come out with successive issues of the same title. Are there any other points of similarity? One way to compare them is to look at what's important about a zine and what's important about a serial. Besides being issued successively, a serial has a recognizable continuity which forms its core, a continuous and structured format, and an assumption of similarity in content from issue to issue. Each issue of a magazine or journal, while it may contain different specific subjects, is structured in the same basic way and the content generally falls within known parameters. Even when a magazine or journal changes its name, the content generally stays more or less the same from issue to issue. For example, the *New Yorker* includes different articles and subjects in each issue, but it's safe to characterize it as a news and lifestyle magazine, and readers can expect that the regular features and basic structure of the publication will remain the same from issue to issue. Moreover, you can assign a subject to the magazine title as a whole and it will be more or less accurate for the length of its run.

On the other hand, I don't think anyone would characterize zines as a format having this core continuity. On the contrary, while some few zines do include the same features repeatedly, on the whole, I think the majority of zines include diverse and unique contents in each issue, and only rarely offer the same type of content on a continuing basis. Some zines might be accurately characterized by broad subject, I'll admit, but there is no guarantee that a zine will have any continuity whatsoever from one issue to the next. As to the question of access, it is possible to assign a subject heading, or headings, to a serial and have that access point be consistent from issue to issue. While "news and information" is not the most descriptive subject heading, and does not indicate specifics, it at least gives an accurate idea of what kind of content is in a "news and information" magazine, and points patrons in a certain direction. It would be virtually impossible to assign a subject heading to a great many zines, unless it was so broad or general as to be almost completely useless. Each zine would be designated a perzine, or a compilation zine, or simply a miscellaneous zine. If the content changes completely from issue to issue, how would you characterize a title except by using the broadest terms?

Some zines are indeed (broadly) consistent in content, but an equal number completely change style and substance with each issue. A zine may keep the same title but change format, contents, subject, approach, or everything from issue to issue. Or the title may change from issue to issue. Or a title may be only a one-shot, with no planned run at all. This makes it hard to equate zines with serials, even though there are a number of similarities. When you look at what counts about serials (the title and content, as stated above) and compare it to what counts about zines (the author, the one aspect that never changes), zines begin to seem further removed from that definition. When you look at the quality of access offered by serials cataloging, you might begin to wonder if there isn't a better way.

So, is it possible that zines resemble books, rather than serials, in spirit and structure? Again, let's look at what is important about a book. A book or monograph, "as opposed to a serial . . . is a work that either is complete as it is issued or has a projected termination point (e.g., an encyclopedia issued in parts)" (*Maxwell's* 117). So a book is a more or less complete work in and of itself (even series books fall under this definition) which is written by one person or a small group of people. The title and subject given for a book (which can be seen as secondary access points) are given *for that work only,* not for all books with that title, all books in a series, all the works by one author, etc. In a book, what is most important, or most prominent, is the author, not the title; the title is simply a tag created by the author. A book is a one-time creation, complete in itself, and it is the creation of an author, all characteristics vital to zines.

The question of access is applicable to books as well. While patrons may look for a book by subject, or by title, or by author, books have the luxury of being cataloged individually. Each individual book is treated separately and patrons can access each individual book in at least three ways. Additionally, any exceptions that occur with zines—multiple authors, unknown author(s), pseudonyms, unknown title, compilations, etc.—are covered under the cataloging rules governing books, whereas there are no rules to cover these exceptions with serials.

At first glance zines seem like serials because that is the format they are based on—they publish periodically, often under the same title with successive chronological designations. But the spirit or essence of zines—what's most important about them—fits more with the way books are defined and treated in cataloging than with the way serials are defined and treated. When looked at as individual creative publications, each individual zine (which is what our collection is based around) suddenly seems a lot more like a book than like an issue of a serial, at least to us.

So we're going to catalog the zines in our collection using a book-type record model. Practically speaking, the only problem for us in using a book model is that we lose the ability to track orders and keep check-in records (which, despite our insistence that zines are like books, are still important since we do order zines individually but very often have more than one issue of a particular title). As I mentioned earlier, however, it was brought to our attention by a perceptive colleague that we could use a standing order record as a second model, which solves that problem and gives us back all the functionality of our beloved Access database. With a standing order we can have a check-in record (masked from the public) and then bibliographic-level records for titles, and then item records for when we have multiple copies of a specific title.

We think that this way we can have it all. The zines get much better subject access if we catalog them as books—we can add notes and contents if we have the time and inclination—and put in subjects and alt subjects based on each particular, individual issue rather choosing just one subject per title. Patrons can search by title, author, or subject, giving them excellent (and unprecedented) access to the collection.

The zines will be shelved in alphabetical order by author (or to say it a different way, in call number order) rather than by subject. So for example, the zine *Book of Letters* would be (I'm making up the cutter number) Zine M255 (for Rich Mackin) bl15 (for *Book of Letters* no. 15). That way each individual zine has its own distinct call number, zines with the same title are shelved together, and the works of one author will be in one spot.

There you have it. Our first attempt at creating an original cataloging system, based on existing standards, for zines. It's too early to know whether or not it will work out as we hope, whether we'll need to make adjustments (I'm sure we will), and whether we're actually on the right track with this strange plan. By the time this book actually comes out I expect we'll know a lot more about what we're doing, and will have some idea how it's going.

NOTE

1. American Library Association, *Anglo-American Cataloguing Rules,* 2nd ed., revised (Chicago: Canadian Library Association, Library Association, American Library Association, 1988).

Spreading the Word

Phew! Well, now that you've organized your zines and are ready to go, it's time to think about spreading the word about your spiffy new collection. Believe me, no one will come looking for it unless you make sure they know it's there; no one is going to come ask if you have zines because, *of course*, you don't. But you do! So while you don't need to come up with an elaborate marketing scheme in order to publicize your collection, you will need a preemptive publicity strategy to alert patrons (and potential patrons) to the fact that you do, surprisingly, amazingly, have zines in the library. There are a couple of things to think about up front, and then a couple more to consider down the road that will help you tailor your publicity and make every flyer count.

Branding

To begin with, I found reading (or at least browsing) through marketing books extremely helpful, given that I didn't really know anything about the finer points of advertising, and I perused as many as I could get my hands on, scanning for ideas that could be adapted to my particular circumstances. One concept that came up again and again was "branding," that is, the process of converting a service, product, or organization (or combinations of the three) into a recognizable brand which in and of itself communicates the essence of what the service, product, or organization stands for or offers. It's a kind of shorthand, I guess. Think of the images, sensations, history, meaning, everything that comes to mind when you see the Disney logo, or even hear the name. Obviously branding is a powerful concept that libraries can (and do) incorporate in order to improve their visibility and reputation.

So while this is neither the place nor the forum to discuss the intricacies of marketing tactics, I think the idea behind branding is relatively simple to extrapolate and apply. Think about what kind of an image (or images) you want your collection to promote and what kind of message you want to send and decide the best way to convey them. I found it helpful to jot down all the concepts or words that came to mind when I thought about zines: words like "freedom," "expression," "creativity," "communication," but also words like "unrestrained," "controversial," "intense," and "strange." I thought about what the purpose of zines was in general, and what their purpose was in the library, and added phrases like "making your voice heard," "letting everyone produce content," and "having something for everyone."

This little exercise helped me pinpoint what was most important to me about the collection and what aspects I wanted to share with others. By narrowing down and cleaning up the lists generated by this brainstorming, we were left with a pretty clear picture of the "essence" we felt it was important to communicate, an idea of what we wanted our "brand" to stand for. At the very least, we had a pretty good idea of what we wanted to say, how, and to whom. When combined with the list of proposed audiences, this was a powerful tool in creating a relevant and attractive "brand" for the zine collection.

Clearly there's no "right" way to market a zine collection. It all depends on what kind of a collection it is, who it serves, and what its purpose is. But thinking about these questions will help you generate ideas that will work, whereas using the same old traditional materials and strategies just might not. Elucidating the concept behind the "brand" is helpful in and of itself, but taking the next step and actually "branding" your collection opens up new possibilities for publicity that make a huge difference.

Audience

Think about who your target (or initial target) audience is by answering the following questions: Who do you think will be the primary users of the collection?

What kinds of zines are in it? Did you focus on teen zines? Is it more of an adult collection? Are you hoping to bring in new patrons who are unfamiliar, or unimpressed, with the library, or is your first priority working with the users you already have? Of course, the answer to all of these questions might be a general yes, which is great. The City Library collection includes all kinds of zines and is designed to be used by teens and adults, to draw in new patrons, and to expand the possibilities for loyal users. The more possible users the better, I say; just make sure you can describe the people you are trying to reach. Break them down into smaller groups and outline the general characteristics of each group: who are they, what do they care about, where will you find them?

Once you've described the group or groups that you want to connect with, start thinking about the different approaches that might work. One detail to consider up front is where your publicity will be taking place. That is, if you are looking to attract new patrons to the library, putting up posters or having flyers available *at the library* is not going to be helpful. They don't frequent the library, so advertising there isn't going to do much good. On the other hand, posters and flyers in the library are exactly the way to reach regular library users.

If you're advertising inside the library, traditional publicity practices will probably work, though you'll still want to cultivate innovative ideas as far as graphics and wording are concerned. Create signage and posters that reflect the spirit and content of zines; one obvious way to capture that "look" is to use a typewriter-style font, clip art, cut-and-paste production, or unusual wording. While this style will definitely convey the stereotypical "zine" look, it's worthwhile to go beyond the standard "zine" format and look at different styles as well. Try other creative approaches: have staff or volunteers or your teen advisory board make flyers advertising the collection. If you really want to capture the individual look of zines, have individuals make the publicity materials and let them choose their own style and wording. Why not have multiple versions of the same flyer or poster, each with its own spin?

This same approach will serve you well when creating publicity materials for distribution outside the library. Taking the multiple flyer concept a step further in hopes of attracting potential patrons, we broke down the "outside the library" group into smaller sections based on where we thought we would find them. Then we created custom flyers for different venues, designed to attract the attention of that particular group. Obviously this is a time-intensive approach, but again, we enlisted volunteers, the teen advisory board, and artistic staff members so the work was spread out. Remember, if you can't do it right, if you can't catch people's attention and attract new users, one of the best reasons for creating this type of a collection goes untapped.

Hence, custom flyers. It was imperative that we bring in new patrons, so allocating time and effort to publicity materials was crucial. We planned to distribute flyers across the city, and made a prioritized list of the places we wanted to visit. Then we got to work. For example, we created one flyer for a local coffeehouse/skateboard shop which played hip-hop music, served vegan food, and catered to a crowd of late teens/early twenties kids, the majority of whom were male. We knew that the place was a gathering spot for graffiti artists as well, so our flyer featured graffiti-type letters, skateboarding slang, and random skateboarding clip art, designed specifically to appeal to the kids who hung out at that venue.

A completely different flyer was created for a local goth-inspired dance club that inhabited an old church near the library. Produced on red and purple paper with black lettering and graphics, this flyer featured a gothic clip-art theme, a spidery inscription, and an invitation to explore the "dark side" of the underground press.

While customized, the flyers weren't necessarily elaborate. Other than stating that we had a zine collection, they simply gave the address and phone number of the library, library hours, and the location of the collection within the building. Some flyers included a brief description of the collection, or a definition of the word "zine," but that was about it. We concentrated more on the look of the flyer than on the amount of information we could squeeze into it. We figured that what was most important was piquing interest, and that this was also the hardest thing to accomplish. Our mission was to create publicity that would stand out, that would catch the attention of potential patrons, and then keep them reading long enough to find out what was being advertised. Whether this was their first encounter with zines or they were seasoned zinesters, we just wanted people to know that we had them. Those who were interested would come visit the collection, and once they were inside the library, there were all kinds of opportunities to transform them into "raving fans," to paraphrase teen librarian extraordinaire Patrick Jones (paraphrasing Blanchard and Bowles).[1]

The point, obviously, is to cater to your audience. Do a little research, ask around, talk to your patrons, your coworkers, your friends, your friends' kids. Whatever it takes, you need to form an idea of what will appeal to the people you're trying to attract. In many cases, the mere fact that they saw a flyer which reflected what they were into changed, if even just a little, potential patrons' idea of the library. After all, something had caught their eye, they'd taken the time to read the fine print, and then they had discovered that this intriguing notice was advertising something *at the library.* Hopefully, curiosity and surprise will propel them right through your front door.

Changing Gears

It's important to note that the brainstorming involved in branding is something that should be revised regularly, and periodic assessment of current and potential patrons is also warranted as your collection grows and changes and takes shape within your community. To illustrate, I again present you with a story about the history of the City Library collection. Once the collection had been around for a while and it was fairly well known that the City Library carried zines, we moved away from customized publicity to a more standardized approach. This shift didn't happen entirely by choice, but we've made it work to our advantage, I think. I'll admit I still miss our haphazard, ultra-creative, multiple flyer approach, but far be it from me not to support the library that allowed the collection to thrive in the first place.

So what happened? Well, at some point during the process of building the new City Library, a design firm was hired to create a "look," a "brand," for the system as a whole that would give the library a higher profile and consistent image within the community. Along with a new logo, City Library publicity materials (including ours) got a new, fairly standardized look, which created continuity and allowed patrons to easily recognize library literature. I'll admit up front that we were more than a little dismayed to find that our days of producing crazy flyers were over, but I'll also admit that it was probably time for us to grow up a bit and move into our new position within the library and the larger community.

The only sticking point for us was that we wanted our own logo. We had actually been toying with the idea for some time by that point, and saw the change in library graphics as an opportunity to look more closely at the possibilities. The biggest question was whether it was indeed appropriate for the zine collection to have its own logo, or whether making that distinction separated the collection too much from the rest of the library system and lessened the impact of the new library look. Of course, as with many steps in the process of building this collection, we didn't really know what we were getting into, and issues arose which, not being experts in this area, we didn't foresee.

There are pros and cons to giving the zine collection that little bit of separation a different logo implies. First, if you're trying to attract library nonusers, a little separation might not be a bad thing, depending on why exactly they don't use the library. If they've had a bad experience, or have a limited view of what a library is, not lumping it all together might be ideal (after all, as I mentioned above, you need to get them through the door before you can change their minds). Second, having a separate logo gives the collection its own identity, which helps with publicity and is nice when you're dealing one-on-one with individuals from around the world. On the minus side, separating the zine collection from the rest of the library introduces that notion of "otherness," discussed way back in chapters 3 and 5, which is something we certainly don't want to promote or endorse. (At the same time, though, "otherness" is exactly what will attract some patrons, so keep that in mind.) The zine collection is part of the library—which is sort of what makes the whole thing cool to begin with—so why not just say so up front by using the same logo? There's also the risk that other departments or groups within the library might follow suit and demand a logo of their very own, which, if allowed, would indeed begin to muddy the branding waters. While I'm still not certain whether having a separate zine collection logo is the best way to go, I think having the discussion was educational, to say the least, and helped us evaluate the current state of the collection and its relationship to the library.

In our particular case, there was quite a bit of (heated) discussion about whether the zine collection should have a separate logo. The possibility of multiple logos—and the effect that would have—was raised and was most definitely seen as problematic. We also weren't sure if it was appropriate to separate the collection from the rest of the entire library system by giving it its own little symbol. Those questions haven't been fully resolved even now, though we did negotiate an arrangement that seems to be working.

Anyway, we *do* have a separate logo for the zine collection (see figure 9.1)—based on the library logo but tweaked just enough to be distinct—that we use sparingly and with permission. The resemblance between the two is obvious (see figure 9.2 to compare), which ties us to the library but also allows us a little independence, a little personality. We don't use the logo on publicity materials produced by our Public Relations Department, for the most part, but are able to take advantage of it when doing publicity outside the area.

One of the benefits of the great logo debate was being able to more clearly appreciate the shift in thinking—both within the library and within the zine collection staff—that's occurred over the life of the collection.

SALT LAKE CITY PUBLIC LIBRARY ZINE COLLECTION

Figure 9.1 City Library Zine Collection Logo

For the first five years we were scrambling to attract new patrons, to be recognized, to get some respect. We felt an intense need to offer potential patrons whatever would seem immediately attractive—in terms of publicity—in order to get them through the door, while at the same time opening their minds to a new vision of libraries. We wanted to spread the word about the collection (and about the myriad possibilities that zines create) to the citizens of Salt Lake City, to members of the zine community, and to all the folks in libraryland. In short, we felt a lot of pressure to cater to various groups in the hope of attracting their attention and their respect.

As we became more established, found our niche, and expanded our patron base, however, we felt less of a need to customize, and more of a need to assert our own identity. Not that we stopped customizing altogether, but our publicity materials definitely reflected our changing position, both within the community and within the larger zine scene. Instead of continually modifying our look to attract potential patrons, we've begun to simply declare who we are and what we offer, secure in the knowledge that we do indeed have a place within the library and within the city of Salt Lake.

I'm not sure what lessons there are to be learned from this, except to say that things change. Don't get stuck in a rut. Do what you need to do in order to get the word out about your collection. If you have to turn cartwheels and offer pink balloons in order to attract patrons, well, do it. But keep in mind that once you become established, it might benefit you to rethink your approach, change the way you publicize, and find a new angle. Not that you'll ever stop catering to your patrons, or to potential patrons—that, in a broad sense, is our job, after all—but given time, a new plan of attack just might be in order.

Steal from Everyone

But where do the ideas come from, the ones you use at the beginning or the ones you substitute later on? Ideas are all around you, and anything that seems like a viable option is one. Steal from magazines (especially magazines geared toward teens) and from the movies, from television and from radio. You can adapt the approach taken by just about any marketing scheme, publicity stunt, or advertising concept, but look further. Look at what your target audience consumes and figure out what appeals to them about it. Then copy it.

For example, reality television is super hot right now, and the concept behind it lends itself perfectly to the voyeuristic quality of zines. Make a flyer or poster that draws parallels between reality television and perzines, or put up a display of your favorite zines and then have patrons "vote one off" each week until you have a winner. Use the release of a new movie based on comic book characters to inspire a comic-style flyer which highlights the independent comics in your collection. (You could also incorporate Free Comic Book Day into this idea, and host a DIY comic workshop—though I should be saving ideas like this for the next chapter.) Both cable television and teen magazine stalwarts like *Seventeen* have embraced the DIY concept, so publicize the fact that zines themselves are DIY with a "make your own" flyer and workshop and set up a display of DIY zines in your collection for patrons to browse.

Use quotes from the zines themselves, or quote from reviews in the manner of movie endorsements. Use comments collected from staff and patrons, like those commercials which feature excited audience members shuffling out of movie theaters. Use popular graphics styles like anime, retro, or hip-hop for inspiration, translating the images and message to fit your collection. Use the zines themselves as a source by looking to your coolest titles for ideas; after all, zinesters are cool, and they do cool stuff, and if you want to be cool, they're a good place to look for inspiration. Anyway, you get the idea. As with all library materials, promotion is crucial, and finding new and innovative and creative approaches to promoting your collection (of zines or books or CDs) is half the fun, for me at least.

Hitting the Street

My final advice on publicity, which I hinted at above, is to go where the potential patrons are; don't expect them (initially, at least) to come to you. If you're looking to attract library nonusers, you'll obviously need to step outside the building and do a little (or a lot of) direct marketing. It's really not that hard, though it does take time and courage. Make a list of all the places you think potential patrons hang out. Prioritize the list by deciding where you'll reach the most people, where you'll have the biggest impact, or which group needs to hear from you the most. Schools are good, but not just junior high and high schools. Hit the community college and technical schools, the university, private schools, even elementary schools. And then look beyond schools altogether because that's really where you want to focus.

Coffee shops, record stores, dance clubs. Art galleries, museums, concert halls. Vintage shops, tattoo parlors, art supply stores. Skate shops, independent bookstores, vegetarian restaurants. Movie theaters, the mall, the skating rink. Go wherever your patrons are. Explain who you are, what you're promoting, and why you thought that particular venue was a good place to do it, and make sure it's all right to pass out literature, hang posters, or leave a stack of flyers. Remember, the person you're talking to about handing out flyers is also a potential patron, so do your best to convince them to check out the collection for themselves.

If possible, leave or distribute something besides flyers—buttons or stickers, for example—something more permanent that patrons will think is cool and which will continue promoting the collection, and the library, long after the flyers have been torn down. Buttons and stickers are "bells and whistles" publicity materials and they're not essential, but if you can find a way to make them happen, it'll be worth your while. If you don't have funds to print up slick stickers for distribution or to purchase a button maker of your own, try one of the distros that will do custom orders, like Microcosm. They're good and cheap and just might make it possible. Imagine binders and folders carried by high schoolers and covered with library-promoting stickers. Think big and imagine bumper stickers. It's definitely an investment, but if you can make buttons to distribute I would highly recommend it, because buttons are fun and they're a staple of the zine community. High school kids, college kids, even so-called adults like me love buttons. Like stickers, the beauty of buttons is that they're out there for all to see; people actually wear them, if not on their clothes, then on their backpacks, jackets, or hats. Think how cool a little zine library logo button (see figure 9.2) would look surrounded by band logos, witty sayings, and random images on

Figure 9.2 City Library and Zine Collection Logo Buttons

some kid's jacket. "Where'd ya get that one?" a friend asks. "It's from the library!" the kid replies, and that implied testimonial—they're wearing a library button!—is literally priceless.

NOTE

1. Ken Blanchard and Sheldon Bowles, *Raving Fans: A Revolutionary Approach to Customer Service* (William Morrow, 1992), as noted by Patrick Jones (and Joel Schumacher) in *Do It Right: Best Practices for Serving Young Adults in School and Public Libraries* (New York: Neal-Schuman, 2001).

ten

Programming
and Outreach

As with virtually every other subject covered in this book, my approach in this chapter is to alert you to some of the options, tell you what's been done at my library, and encourage you to use your own imagination and judgment to go from there. Programming with zines and for zines is fun, and the possibilities are virtually endless—it just requires an open mind, a little creativity, and a willingness to try (or convince someone else to try) something new.

Of course, before you get down to the business of programming, you positively must have an opening day soiree to celebrate your new collection. Invite the media, send out invitations, serve refreshments, provide music. Make up a flyer with details about the collection—why it exists, who it's for, how it works, how (and why) patrons can become involved. If all that seems disproportionately grand for your modest collection, scale it down, but do something, even if you just put up a sign. After all, it's not every day that a library opens a zine collection—believe me, it's not.

At the Library

Once you've made an opening splash, how do you keep the momentum going? Well, let's begin by looking at some of the ways to incorporate zines into programming and displays at the library itself. An informal event like an open house is a fairly stress-free way to publicize the collection, invite patrons to mingle and browse, and make contact with the people in your community who are interested in zines. You can make it as elaborate or as simple as you want; all you really need is a place to hang out, zines to browse, and a sign-up sheet (because you definitely want to get a mailing list going at this point). Add music or snacks as desired, offer up whatever freebies you've collected from zinesters (flyers, sample copies, buttons, stickers), and give away promotional items of your own (booklists, upcoming events), if you've got 'em. That's about it. Simple and effective.

The first couple of events we ever held in conjunction with the zine collection were open houses, held in the evening, in the Periodicals Department where the zines lived. Yes, we pretty much took over an entire corner of the department, but patrons didn't seem to mind (much), and a number of people who hadn't come expressly for the purpose of seeing the collection ended up coming over to see what the fuss was about. In fact, quarterly open houses became something of a tradition for us, at least until we moved to our new building. We gave the series a name ("An Evening Underground," which we thought was incredibly punnish given the subject matter and the fact that the Periodicals Department was two stories below ground level) and we had good turnouts every time.

Based on that success, we held our first do-it-yourself zine workshop ("From A to Zine: Learn How [and Why] to Start Your Own Zine"), a program that became incredibly popular, and one that we present often, both in the library and on the road. In the workshop we spent a short time discussing the history of zines, a little longer describing what they are (and answering all those questions mentioned in chapter 1), and then explained how easy and rewarding it was to start your own. We talked about distros and review zines, ideas for content, tips for format and layout, the cost of photocopying and mailing, and basic zinester etiquette. We provided flyers with lists of contact information, sample copies which patrons could look through to get ideas, and a willingness to answer any and all questions.

Brooke and I were quite frantic before our first workshop, not having any idea what kind of turnout to expect, how we would be received, and whether or not we had prepared appropriate material for the audience. I was pretty sure it was going to be a disaster: either no one would have the slightest idea what we were talking about, or a bunch of hard-core zinesters would show up and jeer us out of the room, disdainful of our rudimentary knowledge of zines (not that they would ever do this, but you know those visions of doom you get just before a program). Or perhaps no one would come at all.

In actual fact, we had a good-sized crowd—about sixty-five people—who were thrilled to hear what we had to share. Some of them knew about zines and were amazed that the library would be putting on a program about them. Many others had no idea what we were talking about, but quickly got the idea and were thrilled to have been introduced to them. We had scheduled an hour for the program (and worried that we wouldn't be able to fill it), but we spent more like two and a half hours presenting, answering questions, talking to people, making connections, and listening to suggestions. All told, a very successful program. Based on that happy experiment, we began holding "make your own zine workshops" on a regular basis, alternating them with the zine open house nights. We eventually moved this program out of the library, too, though we've never stopped offering it there.

Once we'd more or less established ourselves as a collection to be reckoned with, we began hosting guests and offering open mike readings. The first such event featured a couple of Boston-based zinesters, Rich Mackin and Rosie Streetpixie, well-known names in the zine community, who were driving cross-country and agreed to make a stop at the City Library. We went all-out on this one, planning an afternoon session in two parts, and then an evening performance at a local all-ages art space. Geared towards teens but open to anyone (of course), this event was promoted as a way to learn how to get involved, speak up, and act out.

The first afternoon session was a discussion of activism led by Rosie, creator of the zine *One Ear to the Ground* and a sixteen-year veteran, who shared her experiences as an activist and then skillfully facilitated a discussion about the difference an individual can make, how to get people involved in a cause, and how to transform the local activist scene. That was one utterly brilliant hour, and one I will never forget. We had a crowd so large many of us were sitting on the floor, and while many of us just sat back and listened, Rosie actually got quite a discussion going, involving a great many of the teens in the audience. From the comments I received as they left that day, and the e-mails and phone calls I received later on, I know that one program made a huge impact. I'll talk about why I think it struck such a chord in a moment.

The second afternoon session was a more focused version of the "make your own zine" workshop led by Rich, whose zine *Book of Letters* is unarguably one of the most popular and well-known titles around. Rich is also an activist, "corporate poet," and traveling performer, which made for a hilarious and insightful workshop. Having worked at a copy shop for many years, Rich was able to offer tips and tricks for getting the most out of a photocopier machine. At the same time he recounted his experiences with the zine and activist communities, and tied the whole thing together (as we'd hoped) by giving an impromptu speech on the empowering qualities of self-publishing and activism. The audience was enthralled. To this day I think that was one of the best programs we've ever hosted. The fact that it was designed for teens and featured two young, engaging speakers who looked a lot like the kids in the audience didn't hurt. The subject matter, the inclusive presentation, and the passion with which it was presented were the real key, however.

That night most of the afternoon audience reassembled, along with a number of new faces, at a local arts cooperative which had agreed to host a reading for us. It may seem weird that we moved the program from the library to an outside venue, but we wanted to show that the library could sponsor a cool, alternative event in a cool, alternative venue and perhaps attract patrons who wouldn't attend something held at the library itself. We wanted to draw in anyone who was just hanging out in that space and alert them to the fact that we were, in fact, cool. And it worked. People were surprised. And impressed.

After a brief introduction (which included announcing a bunch of upcoming library events including the teen summer reading program, the battle of the bands, and the next zine open house), Rich and Rosie took turns reading from their work (which was also for sale), answering questions, and chatting about their experiences in Salt Lake City. They even put in a good word for the library. After the reading there was much mingling and socializing, lots of zine talk, lots of library talk, and an impromptu planning session with the venue organizers that resulted in at least two other successful programs.

We've had Rich back a number of times since then, as well as numerous other zinesters, including the crew from Microcosm Publishing, Alex Wrekk and Joe Biel (and many of their friends); in the last two years we've hosted both their "Cut and Paste" tour and their "Copy and Destroy" tour, which featured a number of amazing writers, crafters, artists, and poets. We've also welcomed the Mobilivre Bookmobile, a simply astounding traveling museum out of Canada that has to be seen to be believed. (See appendix A for contact information on their trailer, workshops, and tour schedule.) We like to have guests.

Not that we limit our readings to guests, however. We've held a couple of open mike-style programs where local zinesters are encouraged to read from their own work. While popular and fun, this can lead to some interesting—to say the least—performances, so be warned. Unless you state up front that certain subjects or language are restricted, you can be sure that you'll get some of them; depending on your audience at such an event, this may or may not be a problem.

Beyond programming, we've had a lot of fun incorporating zines into other areas of the library, especially in the Teen Department, which, you'll remember, houses its own mini-collection of zines. Probably the most popular zine-inspired innovation is one that I can't even credit properly, since I can't remember where the idea first came from. In any case, the idea was to expand the appeal and use of the booklists we offered in the Teen Department by transforming them into zines. I'll explain. Rather than printing up yet another bookmark-shaped list of historical fiction titles or books about sports, we're using the zine format to give us more space (so we can include more information about each selection) and wider appeal (by offering something unexpected, quirky, and cool).

The subjects for each booklist range from broad (mysteries) to ultra-specific (people with wings), from traditional (award winners) to weird (*A Guide to Irreversible Insanity*—one of my favorites). We have lists that highlight a particular series (the "Abhorsen" books by Garth Nix) or a particular type (books of mythic fiction) or particular theme (ghosts). I hate to say that the possibilities are endless—it's such a cliché and I think I've already said it once in this chapter—but they are. The zine booklists we've done so far are all quarter-size (that is, one quarter of an 8½ × 11 sheet of paper), but we plan to make all sizes eventually; they vary in length from eight pages to over twenty. For the most part, each book on the list gets its own page, which allows for great variety in presentation and content. Some people include a brief synopsis of the plot, facts about the author, or their own mini-review. Some people draw pictures inspired by each title. We've gotten patrons, volunteers, the teen advisory board, and staff involved in these booklists, and they're indescribably fun to make, read, trade, and share and keep forever.

Alex Woolston, booklist zine-maker extraordinaire, offers running commentary, interesting tidbits of information, and sometimes recommendations for songs to accompany each title. For example, the aforementioned *Guide to Irreversible Insanity* (see figure 10.1) features Joyce's *Finnegan's Wake*, Pynchon's *Gravity's Rainbow*, *Spaceboy at Burlap Hall* by Virginia Ironside, Lewis Carroll's poem "Jabberwocky," *Naked Lunch* by William S. Burroughs, and Douglas Copeland's *Girlfriend in a Coma*, each accompanied by a recommended song by rock group The Who. Now that's a list I would never have come up with in a million years! While definitely weird, it might be wise to keep in mind that this booklist was created by an actual teen and that it's gone through three printings already, which says to me that it's time to revisit the notion of traditional booklists. And that the zine booklists were a good idea.

Personally, I find inspiration in the "top five" lists from Nick Hornby's *High Fidelity* (book or movie), the fun facts from VH-1's "Pop-Up Video," and the

Figure 10.1 Zine Booklists: *A Guide to Irreversible Insanity* and *My Top 10 Favorites*

reader reviews from Amazon.com. I add clip art and the occasional "see also" reference, website, or reference book and presto, instant zine booklist. While my own zine booklists are not nearly as clever or creative as Alex's, I have so much fun thinking them up and putting them together that I will never go back to doing traditional booklists again. (Which is not to say that we don't have them available, or that they aren't extremely worthwhile. I just think zine booklists are a lot more fun to put together.)

Beyond the Library

Most of the programming we've done beyond library walls has either been in cooperation with schools, or at events sponsored by various community organizations, or at the zine conference we attend regularly. Over the years we've learned to adapt our preplanned programs to fit different venues, audiences, and expectations. At the core, though, we're still pretty much offering a variation on that original "make your own zine" program. With a few exceptions . . .

School Visits

In an attempt to organize this section I'm just going to move up through the grades, starting with elementary school and ending with college courses. That's right, elementary school! Just last year we were invited to help a class of fifth- and sixth-graders with a semester-long project: to create a zine from start to finish, including figuring out how to reproduce and distribute it (and how to pay for it). The kids are students in an "open classroom" environment at Washington Elementary School in Salt Lake City, which allowed for more leeway, I suspect, than one might normally find in elementary school, though it's not all that different from the traditional classroom. The kids themselves—while extraordinary— were pretty much your average eleven-year-olds, though I have to say I don't remember being anywhere near that articulate or thoughtful when I was that age.

We visited their classroom with a bunch of (age-appropriate) zines, a vague idea of what their assignment would be, and no idea whatsoever of what to expect. After being introduced to the class, I spent about two minutes highlighting the history of zines, did my best to describe them in terms I thought the kids would understand, and then took questions. The kids took to the idea immediately, without any of the hesitation adults usually have about publishing their own work. There was still a flurry of "can I do this?" questions, but the idea that just anyone could do this, that people would actually pay to read what "just anyone" had to say—that they got right away.

I'd been worried about explaining the concept of zines to such a young audience, but I shouldn't have. They were totally into the idea and planning their own creations before I'd even finished my spiel. After my brief presentation I stuck around while the kids looked over the samples I'd brought and asked me thousands of questions—some even zine-related. I didn't have much formal contact with the kids after that, though many of them did visit me at the library to ask questions or check out the zine collection, and they were pretty much on their own as they worked on their zines over the next few months. About four months later I returned to their classroom to see the finished creations, talk with them about the experience, and enjoy a potluck brunch.

We spent the first half hour looking at the finished zines, which were spread out over every available inch of desk space. I only got through about half the zines in that time, but I was stunned. Absolutely, positively amazed. The teacher asked us to form a circle and the kids began by offering comments about each other's work. Then, with a little prompting from the teacher again, they started a discussion of what they had learned, how they felt about their zines, and whether they thought the exercise had been worthwhile. Would they do it differently next time? Would there be a next time? For the majority of them there would be, and yes, they would do things differently. As the discussion wound down one of the kids asked me what I thought of their work. I felt quite stupid, but I really couldn't think of anything to say. I was literally speechless. Those kids made the most brilliant, the most original, the most creative zines I've ever seen. Each one was completely different, a work of art. I stuttered and stammered my way through, praising them to the sky, and I'm not sure they believed that I thought they were as cool as I said they were. So here you have it in print, kids of the open classroom. You made the coolest zines I have ever seen. And you totally proved me wrong—you're the perfect age to teach zine-making to. Absolutely perfect.

Now, this stunning experience was not the first time we'd taken zines to the schools, not by a long shot, and it wasn't the only time I've been left speechless by the experience. Other visits have produced similarly remarkable results, though I don't think I've ever been quite as surprised as I was by those kids. Another group of kids, however, the juniors and seniors of our first visit to Barbara Murdoch's creative writing class at East High School, was equally astounding. We were invited to come in and talk to the class about zines, and I'm pretty certain that this was the first presentation we did outside the library. One of the options for the semester project in the class was to create a zine, so in we came, armed with a bundle of examples, some handouts with copying tips, and a list of upcoming library programs.

Same presentation: history of zines, description of zines, questions from the class, pep talk about the freedom zines offer, the chance for expression, connection with others. I thought it had gone pretty well, and we agreed to come back to later classes to do it all again. A month or so later, however, we started getting e-mails, phone calls, and personal visits from a couple of the girls in the class. They wanted to do something in addition to their project. They wanted to create a "live-action zine" made up of performances: art, readings, drama, music, film, dance. They promised to set the whole thing up if we would just allow them to hold it at the library, away from school, on neutral ground, so to speak (and what librarian would ever turn down an offer like that?). Of course we agreed, though I wasn't sure exactly what they had in mind. Still, it meant that over the next few months we saw a lot of that group, as they planned the event, worked on their zines, and generally hung out at the library. (It wasn't until much later that I found out that a couple of the kids in that group hadn't set foot in a library since they were in elementary school.)

You may have guessed by now that the event they were planning turned out to be the "Make a Racket" zine-inspired talent show I described back in chapter 2. (Fun fact: the title "Make a Racket" was taken from the previous year's teen summer reading program theme—which has since become the unofficial motto of the City Library's Teen Department.) It was an amazing night (even taking into account my sorry tale of cheerleader-inspired narrow-mindedness). One performance in particular (beside hers) really stood out for me: a thin girl with brown dreadlocks who read passionately from her journal-style perzine about the hardships of high school, how she was harassed and tormented, what it was like to have a girlfriend instead of a boyfriend. It was powerful stuff, with language and content that most definitely raised an eyebrow or two. But it was articulate, poetic, heartbreakingly honest, and so brave I was in awe; a tour de force melding of emotion and craft.

Later I received another e-mail from that girl, Moey Nelson, who, as one of the event planners, had been in contact with me for some time previously. She, like many of her classmates, assumed that the library had little to offer her in the way of materials or community, and consequently felt no immediate connection to the idea that, as the American Library Association campaign puts it, libraries change lives. Shortly after the "Make a Racket" program Moey began volunteering at the library, helping with the zine collection, and working on other projects for the Periodicals Department. Just before we moved to the new building, and just after she graduated from high school, I hired her as an aide in the new Level 2 department which housed both the zine collection and the new Teen Department. She sent me the following message, part of which I've shared before, at the end of her first week of work. With her permission I share it in full now:

> Do you realize that you saved my life by coming into my classroom with a stack of zines? I don't think any physical realm could illustrate the vibrancy and anticipation that beamed through my body that day (and every day since). Suddenly, I was like "holy shit! I can do my own thing and not get in trouble!" I look forward to learning about my [new] responsibilities . . . I really do. Because just helping out and doing the small things makes me feel accomplished. And I would also *love* to be a part of the creative process, if possible, discussing what needs to be done about letting people know what zines are, and how they liberate young minds (as well as wiser, more mature minds), working

on (like we were talking about a few weeks ago) not "dealing" with teens, but connecting with them and listening to them. I was thinking today, "whoa, I'm still a teen, how depressing." But then I thought that maybe I could contribute my perspective as someone fresh out of high school. I was asking myself, what is it that I wanted in high school? And I would have to say that it all came down to two things. I wanted a listener and a form of liberating guidance (whether it be writing, painting, or a person that I could trust. But I wanted to feel like it was my choice to make it my guide, instead of someone choosing it for me.) And those things go hand in hand, and they also are Nancy's [the library director] key points for building strong community. So then I was doing cartwheels in my head [imagining the impact I could have by working here]. So yeah, I'm perty happy 'bout all this libary stuff. Sorry to drag this out, I need to learn how to say things blunt and briefly.

To Moey: No you don't. You say things beautifully. I still get all teary-eyed reading it and for me, this is what library work is all about. Not only did Moey gain a new appreciation for the power of libraries to inspire, to connect with teens, to empower them to make good choices, but the library gained Moey, who has contributed in immeasurable ways—both to staff and to patrons—over the past two years. And through Moey we were lucky enough to attract a whole slew of talented and dedicated people—most of whom currently work with me on Level 2 and contribute immeasurably to the collection and to the library. Sniff. Deep breath.

Okay. My final classroom story is so recent it doesn't even have an ending yet, though I suspect it will be successful nonetheless. Less than a month ago Brooke and I visited a typesetting and design class at Salt Lake Community College to present our familiar "make your own zine" material, with a bit of a twist. The instructor, Kerry Gonzales, had come up with the idea of using zines as a way to offer her students a little freedom, a break from the strict guidelines most of her assignments require adherence to. They could choose any subject and any style for this project, though they would be graded on their ability to incorporate the elements of design and their knowledge of typography in the zines they made. As usual, I wasn't really sure how the project would work, but when we arrived in the classroom our questions were answered and fears relieved. The assignment sheet the instructor handed out (see figure 10.2) was so clear and so well thought-out that we saw immediately that the project was not only possible, but actually quite ingenious. We had purposely brought a selection of zines that highlighted different design styles, construction methods, materials, and formats, and we passed them around to the students while doing our traditional song and dance. There were questions about the history of zines,

Zine

NAME_____ DUE DATE_____

OBJECTIVE

Create an original "zine" based on the information given during The City Library presentation.

During the semester, students will work on this project concurrently with other class projects. Throughout the semester, it is the responsibility of the student to make arrangements with the instructor to show project progress and to ask any questions regarding this project.

Grading will foremost be based upon the excellence of the project work: research, creativity, response to the given problem, execution, how completely instructions were followed, project progress, deadline accountability and presentation. This is a semester long assignment and will be graded accordingly.

SPECIFICATIONS

- Design is open. However, design principles and elements, as well as layout and typography guidelines must be followed. Work must reflect an advanced graphic design ability.

- Content is open. However, pornography, offensive language or visuals, and religious or political content is prohibited. If in doubt, ask the instructor. All copy must be original.

- Visuals of some type must be used. Illustrations and photos must be original. Do not use clip art.

- A cover with title and student name (as author) must appear on front.

- Carefully consider your chosen typefaces, shapes, colors, materials, etc.

- Choice of color (ink and paper) is open.

- Choice of paper stock is open.

- Choice of bindery material and method is open.

- Additional items may be added as long as they are securely attached.

- Maximum finished size is 8.5 x 14 inches.

- Minimum finished size is 3.5 x 5 inches.

- Minimum number of pages not including cover is 12.

PROCEDURE

- RESEARCH zines and your subject! A visit to The City Library is highly recommended!

- Consider using the other typography projects from this class as inspiration for your zine.

- Then, begin listing ideas. Start sketching at least ten different thumbnails.

- Choose three different designs from your thumbnails and rough out.

- Have instructor review thumbnails and roughs.

- Choose one rough to work into a tight comp.

- Have instructor review tight comp.

- The computer is highly recommended for this project, however, hand work is necessary in construction and original art.

- Turn in thumbnails, roughs, tights, notes, etc. in an envelope with this project sheet taped on front. Don't forget your name on the project sheet.

- Place student / project information (as required on all projects) on the lower right hand corner of the outside back cover. Include copyright and year. An email site is optional.

- Make two copies for the instructor and two for The City Library. These will not be returned. You might want to make extra copies to trade with other students in the class as well as keep one for yourself.

  Place two copies in one clean envelope marked "For Instructor" and the other two copies in another clean envelope marked " For The City Library." Make sure your name is on each.

- HAVE FUN!

© 2004 Kerry Gonzales, Instructor, Salt Lake Community College

Figure 10.2　Assignment Sheet for the Zine Project, Typesetting and Design Class at Salt Lake Community College about distribution, and about copyright (sharp class!), and then there were questions about the assignment itself.

I have to say that I was terribly impressed with the way Kerry Gonzales structured her assignment, allowing students a great amount of freedom while preserving her ability to grade the finished items using predetermined guidelines. I know the students were excited; many of them stayed after class to talk to us or to ask about specific ideas they already had in mind. And the final sign, for me, that the project is going to have a happy ending was the large proportion of students who showed up at the library the following weekend with more questions, but primarily to browse the zine collection, both for ideas and for fun.

Using zines in the classroom is not a new idea, and it's not a topic I can do justice to here, though I've tried to at least give you a taste. A number of similar projects are on the horizon for us, including zine book reports for a local high school English teacher; another visit to Washington Elementary (this time the fifth-graders are partnering with second-graders, which should be an amazing experience); and a proposed history project which would use the zine format to illuminate assigned historical periods. I do believe that zines can be transplanted successfully to a classroom environment, and that they can adapt to the requirements of grading, but only with careful preparation and a real understanding of the qualities that make zines special. It's imperative to keep the spirit of zines; if there are so many requirements that students get bogged down, what they are creating is not truly a zine, no matter what you call it. I suggest reading the articles listed in appendix A for inspiration and thoughtful analysis, and then, as always, let your imagination run wild.

Zines in the Community

We've taken our presentations and workshops to a number of different venues over the last seven years, and we've been involved with some very cool events such as the Great Salt Lake Book Festival, Salt Lake City's First Night celebration, and CONduit (the area's largest and longest-running science fiction and fantasy convention). We've also partnered with some fantastic organizations like the Job Corps (which provided us with the volunteers that helped get us through our first round of subject classification) and the Volunteers of America, which runs the Homeless Youth Resource Center (HYRC) which sits just blocks from the main library. Our partnership with the HYRC is in its third year now, and the relationship has been wonderful, at least from our viewpoint.

Once again we were approached (isn't it amazing how all these people came to us?) by a staff member at the HYRC whose job it was to come up with afternoon projects for the kids at the center. She oversaw GED study sessions, job skill training, life skills workshops—that kind of thing—and wanted to add something a little more personal, more creative, to the schedule. Her proposal was simple: she would work with the kids on Friday afternoons, sometimes at the center, occasionally at the library, and they would create a zine of their own which we (meaning the library) would then copy. Basically, her kids were interested and willing, but she had no way of producing the zine, having literally no budget for her programs at all. I figured we could most definitely afford to donate paper and toner to such a worthy cause, got permission, and we had a deal.

Most of the kids that frequent the center spend a lot of time at the library anyway (not having anywhere else to go) and were fairly well acquainted with the zine collection as a result. Though it wasn't a formal visit, I'd see them working on zine pages during the week, and on some Friday afternoons, and every once in a while one of them would approach me for feedback or advice or information. After a couple of months, the HYRC staffer arrived at my desk with a sheaf of paper—the first issue of *SLC Streetz* (see figure 10.3). I got to work mak-

Figure 10.3 Issue of *SLC Streetz*, a Zine
Published by Homeless Youths in Salt Lake City

ing a master copy and then made 100 more for them to distribute (plus a couple of extra copies I had their permission to add to the collection).

It wasn't until the next day that I actually found time to sit down and read it, but when I did I was blown away. Within those pages I found a completely different side to the teens who spent so much time in my department. They told their stories, wrote letters to parents or siblings long estranged, offered tactics and advice for surviving on the street, shared poetry and art, and the occasional bad joke. Three years, and a number of issues later, *SLC Streetz* is still going strong, though it publishes irregularly and never looks the same way twice.

I know that many of the kids planned to offer copies for sale on the street, as an alternative to simply asking for change, and if successful (which I'm guessing they were, they're a very persuasive group) I can only imagine the impact reading it would have on the kind souls who bought a copy. I do know what kind of effect *SLC Streetz* has had on me, on other library staff, on patrons who stumble across it in the zine collection, because I've seen people reading it, I've read it and been deeply touched by it myself. I can't really say whether or how making a zine impacted the lives of those kids—many of them come and go so quickly I only see their names in one issue. I like to think that knowing that the library supported their endeavor, and that we valued their voice enough to add it to the library collection, is something that will stick with them in the years to come. I hope they'll always think of the library as a refuge, and remember that we, at least, think they are worthwhile.

Further Afield

Changing the perception of libraries is at the heart of my final example of outreach. But there's a catch: instead of outreach using zines, this time we're doing outreach to zinesters (while at the same time learning a lot ourselves, meeting new people, and immersing ourselves in the zine community for a weekend). I'm talking about zine fairs and other semi-formal zinester gatherings. These gatherings come in all shapes and sizes—fairs, conferences, swap meets, symposia, and more—and offer programming similar to what you would find at a library conference, or a science fiction convention: workshops, panel discussions, demonstrations, networking, and a dealers' room where you can shop for zines, meet the people you've been reading, and pick up all kinds of cool swag. While not feasible or attractive to everyone, if it's at all possible I highly recommend attending any gathering of zinesters your area offers. If you can, travel to one—it will be worth your while.

Brooke and I have attended the Allied Media Conference (formerly the Underground Publishing Conference, or UPC) held at Bowling Green University in Ohio for a number of years now, and we're hoping to make an appearance at this year's PDX (the Portland Zine Fair) as well. We've been invited to present at a number of other events that we haven't been able to manage, though I'm sure someday we'll be in a better position to make the rounds, so to speak. (For a list of zine fairs and conferences, see appendix E.)

Our first experience at the UPC, which I described in chapter 4, was actually quite shocking, as I remember it, in that instead of publicizing our cool new zine collection, we spent much of the weekend proselytizing to unbelievers, sharing the message of libraries, and trying to bring new converts into the fold. We did, I think, convert a few people to libraries, and have increased that number since, but it was shocking to us that we were having to explain libraries to people who we thought would simply embrace us with open arms.

I know I said all this earlier, so I won't belabor the point. Let me just recommend that you investigate the events in your area, or that you could easily travel to, and consider attending or even presenting as soon as you're able. Go prepared, armed with knowledge and zeal, because those zinesters are smart, and they know how to argue, and they enjoy it. And many of them, sadly, shockingly, will not have kind things to say about the library. It's your job to open and change their minds, to initiate them into the grandiose world of libraries, and to help them see the possibilities a partnership with us can create.

Electronic Zine Culture

E-Zines, Blogs, and More

"That's a claim that's already been made for another medium, of course—the one that brought you to this page. In addition to whatever else it is, the Web is zine culture's doppelganger, the j-pegged, java-addled upgrade of a dead-tree, cut-and-paste prototype. As HTML and Photoshop become as accessible as the photocopier, you can expect zines previously published only on paper to move online in droves, and very likely reshape themselves in the Web's image." (Charles Hutchinson, "The View from the Cheap Seats," *Atlantic Unbound*, 18 March 1998, available online at http://www.theatlantic.com/unbound/graffiti/ag9803.htm)

I'm not sure I agree with Hutchinson's statement, so let's get this argument out of the way first. It's fairly obvious that a number of (quite accurate) parallels can be drawn between the Web and the zine scene: both invite participation, both offer a stunning array of voices, both connect people in new and unusual ways. The means to publish, either in print or electronic format, are becoming increasingly accessible to a wider variety of individuals. But to say that the Web will replace print zines, either by publisher choice or reader preference, is to oversimplify and underanalyze both formats; print zines and e-zines are simply not the same creature.

Yes, there is similarity of content; many zine genres—music zines, perzines, political zines—have electronic counterparts, with comparable subject matter. Yes, access to electronic publishing is widespread (though not to the extent often assumed), and publishing on the Web is as easy as publishing a print zine—even easier, in some cases. Yes, the Web has crept into zine culture, transformed it somewhat, and become almost (*almost*) an indispensable means of organizing, communicating, distributing, and informing. And yes, some zinesters have ceased publishing on paper and gone electronic. But not very many of them. I'll admit to the influence the Web has had on zine culture; I'll even embrace it wholeheartedly for all it adds. But I will never accept the notion that electronic zines will replace their material counterparts.

Now this is not to say that zinesters don't use or accept or like the Internet; on the contrary, they have incorporated it into their culture in numerous ways: e-mail, websites, bulletin boards, newsgroups, chat lists. Some zinesters even offer an electronic version of their zine which presents additional content, limited content, or supplements the print version in some way. Some print zines offer select articles or reviews or columns on their website but don't reproduce the entire issue there; some do it the other way around, publishing more on their site than they do in print. In many ways the electronic environment mirrors the zine scene, in that there is the freedom to make your voice heard and the assumption that someone out there wants to read what you've created. As with zines, there are e-zines, sites, lists, boards, and blogs devoted to the most bizarre subjects, the most specific topics, the day-to-day minutiae of life.

But, as noted in chapter 1, there is something about the materiality of zines, about their physical appearance, that is an essential characteristic of the format and an essential element of their appeal. A website can crash or go away. Websites aren't permanent, as anyone who's logged on to check a favorite site only to find it gone can tell you. While print zines come and go, at least there's a permanent record of them, more or less. At this point in time, the Web is not an archive, and there is an impermanence to the electronic realm that just doesn't compare with zines. Besides, not everyone has access to the Internet, but just about anyone can make a zine. So while creating a web page can be just as creative and satisfying, for zinesters, it's not a substitute. A web page and a zine are just not the same thing.

Hutchinson's statement was made six years ago and I see absolutely no indication that it's coming true. If anything, there are more zines out there, and they are more visible and more easily acquired due to the Internet. (In fact, I would say, from my limited perspective, that zine culture is on the verge of another boom, due in no small part to the convenience and speed which the Internet has brought to the scene.) Rather than competing with new technology, zinesters embrace it, put it to use, make it work for them. As Hutchinson himself admits later in the same piece, "As it turns out, zines may have a few things to teach the digital nation about the ideal of a decentralized, democratic medium."

Many zinesters have indeed taken advantage of the additional outlets for creativity the Internet offers, while remaining loyal to their chosen medium. Zinesters have embraced new methods of communication and connection, learning to use the technology to enhance their efforts; after all, they tend toward DIY enterprises anyway, and the Internet seems the perfect environment for their self-directed creativity. In this context, e-zines, blogs, chat lists and boards, and online distros can all be seen as electronic manifestations of zine culture that have influenced, changed, and improved the zine scene, despite claims of its impending demise.

Zinelike Things

E-zines and blogs are two of the most popular electronic outlets, as well as the two which I think most closely resemble their print counterparts. There are a number of excellent books out there on creating and understanding both forms, so I won't dwell too long on them. But it's appropriate to at least define the terms here, look a little more closely at where they fit within the larger zine landscape, and discuss some of the similarities and differences between electronic and print publishing.

E-Zines

An e-zine is simply an electronic zine or magazine. In many, if not most cases, the term is used to mean *any* electronic publication, whether amateur or professional, commercial or nonprofit, and doesn't necessarily indicate a website that actually resembles, in spirit or content, the zines we've been discussing in this book. "E-zine" has sort of a hip ring to it, which explains why it's been more or less co-opted by the professional or commercial electronic community, who use it simply to differentiate electronic publications from print ones; in this case it's just short for "magazine."

I don't know if the distinction is that important anyway, since an amateur website can look just as slick as a commercial one, and a for-profit site can have infinitely better content than a not-for-profit site. There are, as I noted earlier, commercial e-zines as well as personal ones, e-zines that resemble print zines in every aspect but their physicality, and e-zines which look like nothing so much as a glossy, mainstream, newsstand magazine. It's all a matter of semantics. What's important to know about e-zines is that they are electronic, not print, and that they run the gamut with regard to quality, content, subject matter, and ease of use.

Blogs

"As with zines, creating a single source for your life material means you can afford to give it further craftsmanship and aesthetic attention. This can take your diary entries from the night stand to the artistic community, where you are part of a new genre of confessional writing that mixes the personal (and often the mundane) with the literary, the aural, the visual, the interactive." (Michelle Cross, "Dear E-Diary: Public Confessions and Private Doubts," *Broken Pencil* no.14, available online at http://www.brokenpencil.com/features/feature.php?featureid=37)

Blogs (short for "weblogs"), on the other hand, bear little resemblance to a professional or commercial publication of any kind, though some can become pretty widely read. These electronic journals (journal as in diary, not as in periodical) offer writers a new outlet, and readers an unprecedented glimpse into the private lives of others. Basically a blog is an online diary, updated using a web browser, which can be public or passworded for privacy. (For more information, check out www.diaryland.com/faq.html, which offers simple descriptions and explanations applicable to just about any blog.)

So what's the point? Why not just write it all down in a book you keep under your bed? Well, different people have different reasons. Some like having the ability to update friends and family easily. Others simply enjoy the medium. For zinesters, the attraction of blogs may be the chance to try out and perfect new zine material. "A varied and flexible medium, the e-diary is to the Internet what personal zines (or perzines) are to publishing: a chance to use yourself and your life as your principal subject matter," explains writer Michelle Cross in *Broken Pencil*. Or it may be the immediacy that an online diary offers, allowing diarists to skip the layout, proofing, and editing involved in making a paper zine. The electronic environment also mitigates space and distribution constraints.

Zinesters, in particular, also seem to use blogs as a way to communicate not only information about their personal lives, but information about their zine or about upcoming events. Besides, as the Diaryland.com site claims, it's fun.

There are a number of websites (listed in appendix A) which specialize in blogging and offer diarists different display and composition options, levels of customization, and various bells and whistles. For the most part, all that's required is to set up an account and start writing. Most are free, though extra features can be added for a minimal fee. I'd suggest checking out at least a couple of sites to get a feel for stylistic and procedural differences; different blogs have different personalities, and if you're interested in blogging on your own, you'll want to look around for one that calls to you. (On a side note, there are quite a few librarian blogs that are fascinating to read—a list can be found at www.libdex.com/weblogs.html.)

Zinesters Using the Internet

There are a number of other electronic tools that zinesters use to create community, keep connected, and share their wares. Chat lists and online distros are the most obvious, perhaps, but zine websites (including review sites) and online information about zines are also important aspects of the electronic zine scene. As mentioned in chapter 6, chat lists and distros are excellent sources of information and are prime collection development tools. Instructions for joining a couple of excellent zine-related chat lists can be found in appendix A, though a search for zines on the Yahoo! Groups site (www.groups.yahoo.com) will yield numerous other possibilities. A list of distros can be found in appendix D.

Further Information

Contact information for the zines mentioned in each chapter is listed below.

CHAPTER 1

All This Is Mine
Sugene
1709 University Avenue #5
Berkeley, CA 94703
ATIMzine@aol.com

Brainscan
Alex Wrekk
Microcosm Publishing
5307 North Minnesota Avenue
Portland, OR 97217-4551
alex@microcosmpublishing.com

Browsing Room
Tara Moyle
2621 Stuart Avenue #34
Richmond, VA 23220
taramoyle@hotmail.com

Dwan
Donny Smith
P. O. Box 411
Swarthmore, PA 19081-0411

Fragile
Ericka Bailie
P. O. Box 582142
Minneapolis, MN 55458-2142
www.panderzinedistro.com

Ker-Bloom
Artnoose
P. O. Box 3525
Oakland, CA 94609

Kitsch//artificial respiration
Amelia
Available from Vox Populis Distro at
    www.voxpopulis.org

Library Bonnet
Tommy Kovac
1315-I North Tustin Avenue #259
Orange, CA 92867

Low Hug
lowhug@yahoo.com
www.lowhug.blogspot.com for
    current address

Nancy's Magazine
Nancy Bonnell-Kangas
P. O. Box 02108
Columbus, OH 43202

Night Ride Rambling
Kim Buxton
misfitchick@crapmail.com

A Renegade's Handbook to Love and
    Sabotage
Ciara Xyerra
P. O. Box 100
Medford, MA 02153
learningtoleaveapapertrail@
    hotmail.com

Say Cheese
Gil
P. O. Box 112073
Salt Lake City, UT 84147
saycheese@hektik.com

Thoughtworm
Sean Stewart
1703 Southwest Parkway
Wichita Falls, TX 76302-4701

Transom
P. O. Box 77716
Seattle, WA 98177-0716

Twenty-eight Pages Lovingly Bound
    with Twine
Christopher Meyer
P. O. Box 106
Danville, OH 43014

Xenogenesis
Alisa Richter
377 Castle Crest Road
Alamo, CA 94507
crimecaddy@aol.com

Zine Librarian Zine
Greig Means
P. O. Box 12409
Portland, OR 97212
zinelibraries@yahoo.com

CHAPTER 2

All My Stars Are Gone
allmy_stars@msn.com

Frandroid Atreides
P. O. Box 19013
360A Bloor Street West
Toronto, ON
M5S 3C9
Canada
http://greatworm.ca/catalog/
    politics.html

Joe Biel
Microcosm Publishing
5307 North Minnesota Avenue
Portland, OR 97217-4551
joe@microcosmpublishing.com

Book Your Own Fuckin' Life
P. O. Box 460760
San Francisco, CA 94146
www.byofl.org

Davida Gypsy Breier
P. O. Box 963
Havre de Grace, MD 21078
www.leekinginc.com

Broken Pencil
P. O. Box 203
Station P
Toronto, ON
M5S 2S7
Canada
www.brokenpencil.com

Dan Halligan
8315 Lake City Way NE #192
Seattle, WA 98115
http://staff.washington.edu/ten/
ten@u.washington.edu

Matt Holdaway
1945 B Berryman Street
Berkeley, CA 94709-1955
mholdaway@hotmail.com

Ailecia Ruscin
P. O. Box 297
Lawrence, KS 66044
ailecia@hotmail.com

Stephanie Scarborough
P. O. Box 715
Weatherford, TX 76086
http://diystore.cjb.net/

Sean Stewart
1703 Southwest Parkway
Wichita Falls, TX 76302-4701

Teri Vlassopoulos
17 Mountbatten Road
Weston, ON
M9P 1Z1
Canada
vlass@interlog.com

Cat's Claw Herbal, Firewood, Compost This, Dwelling Portably, Arts and Crafts Revolution, A Rough Guide to Bicycle Maintenance, and *Stolen Sharpie Revolution* are all available from Microcosm Publishing, at www.microcosmpublishing.com.

CHAPTER 3

Counterpoise
Charles Willet
1716 SW Williston Road
Gainesville, FL 32608-4049
www.civicmediacenter.org/counterpoise
willet@liblib.com

The American Library Association's *Library Bill of Rights* is available online at http://www.ala.org/Content/NavigationMenu/Our_Association/Offices/ Intellectual_Freedom3/Statements_and_Policies/Intellectual_Freedom2/ Library_Bill_of_Rights.htm.

"The Freedom to Read" statement, a joint statement of the American Library Association and the Association of American Publishers, is available online at http://www.ala.org/Content/NavigationMenu/Our_Association/Offices/ Intellectual_Freedom3/Statements_and_Policies/Freedom_to_Read_ Statement/freedomtoread.htm.

CHAPTER 4

Contact information for the Allied Media Conference is available in appendix E.

CHAPTER 5

Alternative Press Index
Alternative Press Centre
P. O. Box 256
College Park, MD 20740

Alternative Press Review
C.A.L. Press
P. O. Box 1446
Columbia, MO 65205-1446

Alternative Publishers of Books in North America (1995)
Byron Anderson
American Library Association, Social Responsibilities Roundtable
Crisis Press

Annotations: A Guide to the Independent Critical Press (1999)
Marie F. Jones, Charles D'Adamo, Beth Schulman, and Les Wade (Editors)
Alternative Press Centre

CLMP Directory of Literary Magazines and Presses (2003)
Council of Literary Magazines and Presses
Manic D Press

Counterpoise
Charles Willet
1716 SW Williston Road
Gainesville, FL 32608-4049
www.civicmediacenter.org/ counterpoise
willet@liblib.com

Directory of Small Press/Magazine Editors and Publishers, 34th ed., 2003–2004
Len Fulton (Editor)
Dustbooks
P. O. Box 100
Paradise, CA 95967

Factsheet Five is no longer published

Gila Queen's Guide to Markets
P. O. Box 97
Newton, NJ 07860-0097
http://free-path.org/gilaqueen

International Directory of Little Magazines and Small Presses, 39th ed., 2003–2004
Len Fulton (Editor)
Pushcart Press

Pander Zine Distro
Ericka Bailie
www.panderzinedistro.com

*Psychotropedia: A Guide to
Publications on the Periphery*
(1998)
Russell Kick
Pluto Press

*A Reader's Guide to the Underground
Press*
Jerianne
P. O. Box 330156
Murfreesboro, TN 37133-0156
www.undergroundpress.org
jerianne@undergroundpress.org

Scavenger's Newsletter is no longer
published

Small Press Review
Dustbooks
P. O. Box 100
Paradise, CA 95967

Xerography Debt
Davida Gypsy Breier
P. O. Box 963
Havre de Grace, MD 21078
davida@leekinginc.com
www.leekinginc.com

Zine Guide
P. O. Box 5467
Evanston, IL 60204
www.zineguide.net

CHAPTER 6

Fish Piss
Lois Rastelli
P. O. Box 1232
Place d'Ames
Montreal, QC
H2Y3H2
Canada
fishpiss@canada.com

Fucktooth
Jen Angel
jen@clamormagazine.org

Mr. Peebody's Soiled Trousers
Jay Koivu
P. O. Box 931333
Los Angeles, CA 90093

CHAPTER 7

Independent Publishing Resource
Center
917 SW Oak Street #218
Portland, OR 97205
Phone/Fax: 503.827.0249
www.iprc.org
library@iprc.org
info@iprc.org

Zine Librarian Zine
Greig Means
P. O. Box 12409
Portland, OR 97212
zinelibrarian@yahoo.com

CHAPTER 8

Maxwell's Handbook for AACR2R: Explaining and Illustrating the "Anglo-American Cataloguing Rules" and the 1993 Amendments (1997)
Robert L. Maxwell and Margaret F. Maxwell
American Library Association

Muuna Takeena
Tim Palonen
Oritie 4 C24
FIN-01200 Vantaa
Finland

Say Cheese
Gil
P.O. Box 112073
Salt Lake City, UT 84177
saycheese@hektik.com

CHAPTER 9

Dr. Don's Buttons is my favorite place for button makers and button parts. They have excellent prices and even more excellent customer service. See their site at www.buttonsonline.com for more information.

Free Comic Book Day
www.freecomicbookday.com/

Microcosm Publishing
5307 North Minnesota Avenue
Portland, OR 97217-4551
www.microcosmpublishing.com

CHAPTER 10

Joe Biel
Microcosm Publishing
5307 North Minnesota Avenue
Portland, OR 97217-4551
joe@microcosmpublishing.com

Rich Mackin
www.richmackin.org

Mobilivre Bookmobile Project
www.mobilivre.org
info@mobilivre.org

Rosie Streetpixie
rosiestreetpixie@hotmail.com

Alex Wrekk
Microcosm Publishing
5307 North Minnesota Avenue
Portland, OR 97217-4551
alex@microcosmpublishing.com

For more information on using zines in the classroom, do an Internet search for "zines in the classroom," or see the following articles:

Frazier, Dan. "Zines in the Composition Classroom." *TETYC (Teaching English in the Two Year College)* 28, no. 1 (1998).

Knobel, Michele, and Colin Lankshear. "Cut, Paste, and Publish: The Production and Consumption of Zines." Paper presented at the "State of the Art Conference," Athens, Ga., January 2001. Available online at http://www.geocities.com/c.lankshear/zines.html and included in *Adolescents and Literacy in a Digital World*, ed. D. Alvermann, New Literacies and Digital Epistemologies 7. New York: Peter Lang, 2002.

Williamson, Judith. "Engaging Resistant Writers through Zines in the Classroom." Speech delivered at the College Composition and Communication Conference, annual convention in Nashville, Tenn., March 1994. Available online at http://www.missouri.edu/~rhetnet/judyw_zines.html.

CHAPTER 11

E-Zines

An impressive list of e-zines was maintained by John Labovitz until May 2003. While not completely current, it's still an excellent source of information and can be found online at www.meer.net/~johnl/e-zine-list/.

Blogs

The following are a few suggestions for further reading on blogs:

Blood, Rebecca. *The Weblog Handbook: Practical Advice on Creating and Maintaining Your Blog.* New York: Perseus, 2002.

Editors of Perseus Publishing. *We've Got Blog: How Weblogs Are Changing Our Culture.* New York: Perseus, 2002.

Stauffer, Todd. *Blog On: Building Online Communities with Weblogs.* New York: McGraw-Hill, 2002.

Stone, Biz. *Blogging: Genius Strategies for Instant Web Content.* New Riders, 2002.

An incomplete list of blogging sites is as follows:

www.angelfire.com

www.diarist.net

www.diaryland.com/

www.globo.org

www.livejournal.com/

www.metajournal.net

www.mydeardiary.com

www.new.blogger.com/

www.opendiary.com

www.pitas.com/

www.scribble.nu

www.zanga.com/

Chat Lists

In order to join a group you must first register for a free Yahoo account. To go straight to the Yahoo directory of zine-related lists, try http://dir.groups.yahoo .com/dir/Entertainment___Arts/Humanities/Books_and_Writing/Publishing/ Zines?show_groups=1.

My favorite, indispensable lists are:

zinegeeks: http://groups.yahoo.com/group/zinegeeks

zinelibrarians: http://groups.yahoo.com/group/zinelibrarians

zinesters: http://groups.yahoo.com/group/zinesters

Also of interest is the alt.zines newsgroup, which can be found at http:// groups.google.com/groups?oi=djq&as_ugroup=alt.zines.

Distros

A list of distros can be found in appendix D.

Information about Zines

Chip Rowe's excellent site, www.zinebook.com, offers an amazing array of links, articles, and information on zines. Zine resources provided by librarian

Chris Dodge can be found at the Zineology site, www.geocities.com/SoHo/ Cafe/7423/zines.html, and at the Street Librarian site, http://www.geocities .com/SoHo/Cafe/7423/?source=zinebook. In addition, online sites for review zines like *Xerography Debt* and *A Reader's Guide to the Underground Press* offer a wealth of information.

How to Start
Your Own Zine

1. Think of an idea for a zine.
2. Think of a name for your zine.
3. Figure out what you want your zine to look like.
4. Start writing.
5. Layout your zine.
6. Copy your zine.
7. Distribute your zine.

Obviously, there's a lot more that goes into making a zine, but those are the basic steps. There are many questions that are worth asking and answering along the way, such as what do I want to say? How do I want to say it? What do I want it to look like? Who do I want to read it? How will I get it to them? But really, making a zine is a simple and creative act, and I don't think it needs to be made more difficult than it really is. Still, if you'd like more information, it might be worthwhile to spend time looking at some of the in-depth guides available in the books listed in appendix H, or online at some of the sites listed in appendix A for chapter 11. I'd also recommend checking out Rich Mackin's "Copy Centers Are Your Friend," available from www.richmackin.org, which offers invaluable tips and tricks for copying your zine.

Review Zines

Zines that primarily review other zines:

Broken Pencil
P. O. Box 203
Station P
Toronto, ON
M5S 2S7
Canada
www.brokenpencil.com

A Reader's Guide to the Underground Press
Jerianne
 P. O. Box 330156
Murfreesboro, TN 37133
www.undergroundpress.org/

Xerography Debt
Davida Gypsy Breier
P. O. Box 963
Havre de Grace, MD 21078
www.leekinginc.com/xeroxdebt/

Zine Guide
P. O. Box 5467
Evanston, IL 60204
www.zineguide.net/

Other publications that include zine reviews:

10 Things
8315 Lake City Way NE #192
Seattle, WA 98115
www.10things.com/10things

Alternative Press Review
P. O. Box 4710
Arlington, VA 22204
www.altpr.org

Free Press Deathship
P. O. Box 55336
Hayward, CA 94545

Frictionmagazine.com
277 Luedella Court
Akron, OH 44310
www.frictionmagazine.com

Indy Unleashed
Owen Thomas
P. O. Box 9651
Columbus, OH 43209
www.people.delphi.com/vlorbik
vlorbik@delphi.com

Maximum RnR
P. O. Box 460760
San Francisco, CA 94146-0760
www.maximumrnr.com

New Pages Zine Reviews
Sean Stewart
www.newpages.com/
      magazinestand/zines/default.htm

The Poopsheet
Ricko Bradford
P. O. Box 2235
Fredricksburg, TX 78624
http:// P. O.opsheet.blogs P. O.t.com

Punk Planet
4229 North Honore
Chicago, IL 60613
www.punkplanet.com

Slug & Lettuce
P. O. Box 26632
Richmond, VA 23261
chris1slug@hotmail.com

Utne Reader
1634 Harmon Place
Minneapolis, MN 55403
www.utne.com

The Whirligig
Frank Marcopolos
4809 Avenue N #117
Brooklyn, NY 11234-3711
www.thewhirligig.com/index.html

Wonka Vision Magazine
P. O. Box 63642
Philadelphia, PA 19147
www.wonkavisionmagazine.com

Zine Thug
Marc Parker
2000 NE 42 Avenue #221
Portland, OR 97213
www.zinethug.com

Be sure to check out:

The Whizzbanger Guide to Distros
Shannon Colebank
Whizzbanger Productions
P. O. Box 5591
Portland, OR 97228

UNITED STATES AND CANADA

Armadillo Distro
9 Wood Road
Tannersville, PA 18372
http://dizzy.at/dillo
dillodistro@yahoo.com

Black Panther Distribution
274 E Broadway
Winona, MN 55987
www.wakeup.to/bpdistro
bpdistro@mail.com

Brat Grrrl Distro
P. O. Box 2242
Fullerton, CA 92822
www.geekthegirl.net/raynegrrrl
bratgrrrldistro@yahoo.com

bRoken distRO
620 Landry Avenue NW
Albuquerque, NM 87120
www.geocities.com/
    theworldisbroken/distro.html
pukezine@hotmail.com

CS Tiendita
Noemi Martinez
1018 Rosehill Avenue #B
Durham, NC 27705
www.chicanastuff.com
noemi@chicanastuff.com

Deranged Distro
Dann Berg
P. O. Box 5894
Scottsdale, AZ 85261
www.derangeddistro.com
drangeddan@hotmail.com

Dreamer's Distro
P. O. Box 281
Vernon, CT 06066
www.dreamersdistro.com
dreamersdistro@yahoo.com

Driving Blind Distro
c/o Erin
P. O. Box 656
Keyport, NJ 07735
www.drivingblind.org/dbdistro.com
erin@drivingblind.org

Drown Soda
Sara Jane
www.angelfire.com/zine2/drownsoda1
drownsoda@hotmail.com

Echo Zine Distro
Michelle
P. O. Box 11102
Shorewood, WI 53211
www.geocities.com/echozinedistro
echozinedistro@yahoo.com

Existo Distro
Shosh C.
P. O. Box 6924
Portland, OR 97228-6924
http://geocities.com/existodistro
existodistro@yahoo.com

Fortune Cookie Distro
Xiaowei
c/o J Donahue English Department
80 Skillings Road
Winchester, MA 01890
www.fortunecookiedistro.cjb.net
fortunecookiedistro@hotmail.com

Girl+distro
Chelsea
705 Walnut Street
Meadville, PA 16335
www.undoonga.com/~sassafras
sassafras@undoonga.com

Goldman Distro
Vera
128 Glezen Lane
Wayland, MA 01778
www.geocities.com/goldmandistro
cowspop7up@hotmail.com

Great Worm Express Distro
Frandroid Atreides
P. O. Box 19013
360A Bloor Street West
Toronto, ON
M5S 1X1
Canada
http://greatworm.ca
distro@greatworm.ca

Grrrlstyle Distro
www.grrrlstyle.org

Grub Records
P. O. Box 11688
Portland, OR 97211
grubrecords@hotmail.com

Loop Distro
Billy
1357 West Augusta #1
Chicago, IL 60622
www.loopdistro.com
zines@fastworks.com

Mad People Distro
Jen Venegas
4434 Huddart Avenue
El Monte, CA 91731
www.madpeople.com
jen@madpeople.net

Makaiju Distro
Suzilee Hough
P. O. Box 20370
San Jose, CA 95160
www.makaiju.net/distro
leelee@makaiju.net

Mamas Unidas Distro
P. O. Box 3344
Baltimore, MD 21218
www.geocities.com/
   mamasunidasdistro
mamasunidasdistro@yahoo.com

Microcosm Publishing
5307 North Minnesota Avenue
Portland, OR 97217-4551
www.microcosmpublishing.com
joe@microcosmpublishing.com

Moon Potatoes Distro
Amanda
P. O. Box 93937
Los Angeles, CA 90093
www.geocities.com/
   moonpotatoesdistro
moonpotatoes@hotmail.com

Moonlight Requisition Distro
9804 Cardinal
La Porte, TX 77571
http://home.houston.rr.com/sab-
   byjunk/index.htm
sabby_darling@hotmail.com

Moxie Distro
Britt
P. O. Box 210814
Nashville, TN 37221
http://moxiedistro.i8.com
hollyhox@comcast.net

Offbeat Distro
Lorimay
1512 Greystone Drive
Gurnee, IL 60031-9128
www.geocities.com/offbeatdistro
sewn_in_stars@hotmail.com

Operation Kitty Kitty
Katrina
P. O. Box 230356
Boston, MA 02123-0356
www.operationkittykitty.com

Pander Zine Distro
Erica Bailie
P. O. Box 582142
Minneapolis, MN 55458
www.panderzinedistro.com
distro@panderzinedistro.com

Paper Explosion Distro
Marie Abbondanza
   1940 Liacouras Walk #313e
   Philadelphia, PA 19122
www.craftyass.com
marie@craftyass.com

Pleasant Unicorn
Stephanie
P. O. Box 175
Weatherford, TX 76086
http://diystore.cjb.net

Quidgee! Productions
Becky
P. O. Box 641786
Omaha, NE 68164
www.quidgee.com
mail@quidgee.com

The Raucous Tea Party
Sally and Candice
www.geocities.com/raucousteaparty
theraucousteaparty@yahoo.com

SexahKitty Distro
Alex
3713 Bee Creek Road
Spicewood, TX 78669
www.plastichalo.net/sexahkitty
carebearsbraveheart@yahoo.com

Spy Kids Distro
Pixie
508 Whispering Oaks
Moore, OK 73160
www.skdistro.cjb.net
Killgirl81@aol.com

Starfiend Distro
Jenn Starfiend
988 Fulton Street #213
San Francisco, CA 94117
www.starfiend.com
jenn@starfiend.com

Static Cling Distro
P. O. Box 20083
RPO Beverly
Edmonton, AB
T5W 3P8
Canada
http://dork.com/static-cling
static-cling@dork.com

Stickfigure Distro
P. O. Box 55462
Atlanta, GA 30308
www.stickfiguredistro.com
info@stickfiguredistro.com

Super Nova Zine Distro
Meredith
130 Cypress Avenue
Kentfield, CA 94904
www.violeteyes.net/supernova
licoricewhip@bust.com

Sweet Cherry Distro
candy.grrrl
P. O. Box 1176
New York, NY 10018
www.pinkpoodlezine.com/distro
candy.grrrl@pinkpoodlezine.com

Tastes Like Newsprint Distribution
6 South Barn Road
Hopkinton, MA 01748
www.tasteslikenewsprint.tk
TastesLikeNewsprint@hotmail.com

Tomatoes Equal Love
111 West Archer Place
Denver, CO 80223
tomatoeslove@yahoo.com

Valiant Death Records &
Distribution
3337 Poplar Drive
Smithfield, VA 23430
www.valiantdeath.com
valiantdeath@hotmail.com

Wingless Zine Distro
Sarah Bee
47 Ironwood Street
Islip, NY 11751-1913
www.wingless.xexix.net
sara_the_bee@hotmail.com

Xerox Revolutionaries
P. O. Box 3411
Tallahassee, FL 32315-3411
www.hosted.worldwidepunks.net/
xerox_revolutionaries
xeroxrevdistro@yahoo.com

Youth in Revolt Distro
Megan
P. O. Box 268
Loleta, CA 95551
www.youthinrevoltdistro.com
theantifi@hotmail.com

INTERNATIONAL

Fatcheeks Distro
P. O. Box M182
Missenden Road
NSW 2050
Australia
phat@glokenpop.com

Livinghood Distro
Bonnie
P. O. Box 44174
Shaukeiwan Post Office
Hong Kong
http://distro.livinghood.net
distro@livinghood.net

Moon Rocket Distribution
Moira
P. O. Box 7754
Wellesley St.
Auckland, New Zealand
www.moonrocket.co.nz
moira@moonrocket.co.nz

Paperclip Distro
Ursula
E-mail for full address
http://paperclip.binario.org
cinematicsigh@yahoo.com

Passionate Resistance Zine Distro
Markus Kampschneider
Metzer Strasse 58
48151 Muenster
Germany
www.cutekidszines.de.vu
itshardertotell@gmx.net

Red Letter Zine Distro
P. O. Box 14562
Kilbirnie, Wellington,
New Zealand
The_mystery_set@hotmail.com

Smitten Kitten
Kristy
P. O. Box 1219
Camberwell
VIC 3124
Australia
www.smittenkitten.net
smittenkitten@ozemail.com.au

You and Me
P. O. Box 18
40315 M. Sredisce
Croatia
Europe
www.actnow.hr
youandmepress@net.hr

Vox Populis Zine Distro
Amelia
P. O. Box 253
Roselands, Sydney, NSW 2196
Australia
www.voxpopulis.org
voxpopulis_@hotmail.com

This is by no means a complete list, and some contact information may be out-dated. More distros (and current contact information) can be found by simply doing an Internet search for "zine distros," by checking the listings in *Stolen Sharpie Revolution,* or by purchasing *The Whizzbanger Guide to Distros.*

Zine Fairs and Conferences

appendix e

The following is a list of regularly scheduled events; see the individual websites or write the organizers for more details and for exact dates. There are also a great many other events held each year, so check out www.undergroundpress .org/events.html, www.zinebook.com/directory/zine-events.html, or ask one of the zine chat lists for updated information.

Allied Media Conference
Bowling Green University
www.clamormagazine.com

Alternative Press Expo
www.comic-con.org/Pages/
    APEWhatsNew.html

Ladyfest is an event held in many locations around the country. An Internet search on "Ladyfest" will usually bring up the current schedule.

New Jersey Zine Fest
Rutgers University
www.njzinefest.com
njzinefest@yahoo.com

Providence Zine Fest
ProvidenceZineFest@hotmail.com

Portland Zine Symposium
P. O. Box 5901
Portland, OR 97228-5901
www.pdxzines.com

Contact information for selected zines libraries is below; this list is by no means complete. Please see the *Reader's Guide to the Underground Press* website for an updated list of libraries and collections at www.undergroundpress.org/ infoshops-us.html, or Chip Rowe's zine library list at http://zinebook.com/ resource/libes.html.

ABC No Rio Zine Library
Jess, Miranda, or Robynn
156 Rivington Street
New York, NY 10002
zine@abcnorio.org

Alternative Media Library
c/o Michelle Chen
P. O. Box 200077
New Haven, CT 06520

Austin Zine Library
www.geocities.com/
   theaustinzinelibrary/

Autonomous Zone
1573 North Milwaukee Avenue #420
Chicago, IL 60622
www.azone.org

Bard Zine Library
Elissa Nelson
Bard College
Annandale-on-Hudson, NY 12504

Barnard College Collection
Jenna Freedman, MLIS
Barnard College
3009 Broadway
New York, NY 10027

Bread & Roses Library and Infoshop
Community Arts & Media Project
P. O. Box 63232
St. Louis, MO 63163
www.stlcamp.org/bread_rose.html
lilyofthegutter@yahoo.com

BRYCC House Zine Library
1042 Bardstown Road
Louisville, KY 40204
brycc@brycchouse.org

Che Café Collective
Zine Library
9500 Gilman Drive
Student Center B-0323C
La Jolla, CA 92093
http://checafe.ucsd.edu/zines.html

Chicago Great Lakes Underground
   Press Collection
Kathryn DeGraff
DePaul University Library
2350 North Kenmore
Chicago, IL 60614
www.lib.depaul.edu/speccoll/guides/
   upc.htm

Civic Media Center Zine Library
1021 West University Way
Gainesville, FL 32601
www.civicmediacenter.org

CORE Infoshop
P. O. Box 14531
St. Petersburg, FL 33730
www.core-info.org

Darby Romeo Collection of Zines
Alfred Willis
UCLA Arts Library
2250 Dickson Arts Center
Los Angeles, CA 90024

Denver Zine Library
Jamez and Kelly
111 W Archer Place
Denver, CO 80223
www.geocities.com/denverzinelibrary
tomatoeslove@yahoo.com

Independent Media Center
218 West Main Street, Suite 110
Urbana, IL 61801
www.ucimc.org

Insight Infoshop
P. O. Box 1151
Eau Claire, WI 54702
infoshop@angelfire.com

Labadie Collection
Julie Herrada
711 Harlan Hatcher Library
University of Michigan
Ann Arbor, MI 48109
jherrada@umich.edu

The Little Magazine Collection
Andrea Grimes
San Francisco Public Library
100 Larkin Street, 6th Floor,
San Francisco, CA 94102
andreag@sfpl.org

Michigan State University
Randy Scott
Special Collections Division
100 Library
East Lansing, MI 48824-1048
www.lib.msu.edu/comics

Minneapolis Community and
  Technical College Library
Library Zine Collection
1501 Hennepin Avenue
Minneapolis, MN 55403
http://db.mctc.mnscu.edu/library/
  pages/altpress.htm

Olympia Zine Library
115 E 4th Ave
Olympia, WA 98501

Pittsburgh Zine Library and Archive
Deanna Hitchcock
P. O. Box 8131
Pittsburgh, PA 15217

Pond Zine Library
324 14th Street
San Francisco, CA 94103
www.mucketymuck.org

Popular Culture Library
William T. Jerome Library
Bowling Green State University
Bowling Green, OH 43403
www.bgsu.edu/colleges/library/pcl/
  pcl.html

Richard Hugo House
Zine Archive Project
1634 11th Avenue
Seattle, WA 98122
www.hugohouse.org

Safe Haven Zine Library
Mark Tristworthy
P. O. Box 4491
Austin, TX 78765

Salt Lake City Public Library
Julie Bartel
210 East 400 South
Salt Lake City, UT 84111
jthomas@slcpl.lib.ut.us

San Diego State University
West Coast Zine Collection
  5500 Campanile Drive
San Diego, CA 92182-8050
http://infodome.sdsu.edu/about/
  depts/spcollections/rarebooks/
  zinesfindingaid.shtml

The Sarah Dyer Collection
Sallie Bingham Center for Women's
  History and Culture
Amy Leigh
Special Collections Library
Duke University
Durham, NC 27708-0185
http://scriptorium.lib.duke.edu/
  women/newsletter/issue01/
  page4.html

University of Montana
Chris Mullin
Mansfield Library Small Press
  Collection
32 Campus Drive, #9936
Missoula, MT 59812-9936

Stores That Carry Zines

The following stores carry (or have carried) at least a small selection of zines:

Atomic Books
1100 West 36th Street
Baltimore, MD 21211
www.atomicbooks.com

Boxcar Books
310A South Washington Street
Bloomington, IN 47401-3529
www.boxcarbooks.org

City Lights Bookstore
261 Columbus Avenue at Broadway
San Francisco, CA 94133
www.citylights.com

Comic Relief
2138 University Avenue
Berkeley, CA 94704
www.comicrelief.net

Idle Kids Books and Records
3535 Cass Avenue
Detroit, MI 48201
www.idlekids.com

Iron Feather Book + Zine Shop
P. O. Box 1905

Boulder, CO 80306
www.ironfeather.com

Left Bank Books
92 Pike Street
Seattle, WA 98101
www.leftbankbooks.com

Powell's Books
1005 W. Burnside
Portland, OR 97209
www.powells.com

Quimby's
1854 W. North Avenue
Chicago, IL 60622
www.quimbys.com

Reading Frenzy
921 Southwest Oak Street
Portland, OR 97205
www.readingfrenzy.com/

Wooden Shoe Books
508 South Fifth Street
Philadelphia, PA 19147
www.woodenshoebooks.com

Angel, Jen, editor. *Zine Yearbook* (Volumes 1–7). Soft Skull. See www.clamormagazine.com for more information.

Block, Francesca Lia, and Hillary Carlip. *Zine Scene: The Do It Yourself Guide to Zines.* Girl, 1998.

Brent, Bill. *Make a Zine.* Black Books, 1997.

Farrelly, Liz. *Zines.* Booth-Clibborn Editions, 2001.

Friedman, R. Seth. *The Factsheet Five Zine Reader.* Three Rivers, 1997.

Gunderloy, Mike. *The World of Zines: A Guide to the Independent Magazine Revolution.* Penguin, 1992.

Potter, Jeff. *Out Your Backdoor: A Zine Anthology.* Out Your Backdoor, 2001.

Rowe, Chip, editor. *The Book of Zines: Readings from the Fringe.* Henry Holt, 1997.

Sabin, Roger, and Teal Triggs, editors. *Below Critical Radar: Fanzines and Alternative Comics from 1976 to Now.* Codex Books, 2002.

Taormino, Tristan, and Karen Green, editors. *A Girl's Guide to Taking Over the World: Writings from the Girl Zine Revolution.* St. Martin's, 1997.

Vale, V., editor. *ZINES! Volume One: Incendiary Interviews with Independent Publishers.* Re-Search, 1999.

Vale, V., editor. *ZINES! Volume Two.* Re-Search, 1999.

INDEX

Julie Bartel is teen librarian and systemwide selector of teen materials and graphic novels at the Salt Lake City Public Library. A long-time advocate of and participant in the alternative press, she is also the founder and coordinator of the City Library zine collection, arguably the oldest and largest of its kind in a public library. In 2003 Bartel was awarded the Beginning Professional Award for Teen Services by the Mountain Plains Library Association. She graduated from the University of Utah and earned her M.L.S. degree from Syracuse University.